THEORY

OF

ARCHES.

BY

Prof. W. ALLAN,

Formerly of Washington and Lee University, Lexington, Va.

NEW YORK:
D. VAN NOSTRAND, PUBLISHER,
23 MURRAY AND 27 WARREN STREET.
1874.

THEORY OF ARCHES.

The following is an amplification and explanation of Professor Rankine's chapters on this subject.

Perhaps the clearest way of developing the "Theory of Arches" is to begin with the consideration of the forces which act upon a suspended chain or cord. The force in the chain or cord is just the opposite of that upon an arch—that is, it is *tension* instead of *compression*, but the relations between the "external" and "internal" forces, or what is the same, between the loads and the resistances they produce, are strictly analogous.

Let C A B (Fig. 1) be a cord suspended at C and B and loaded in any manner over its whole length. Consider the forces acting on this cord. Suppose it attached to a hook at B and to another at C. A cord without stiffness cannot exert a pull except in the direction of its length: therefore the "pulls" in the rope at C and B, and exerted at these points on the suspending hooks, must be in the direction of the tangents at those points. The load is supposed to be

FIG. 1.

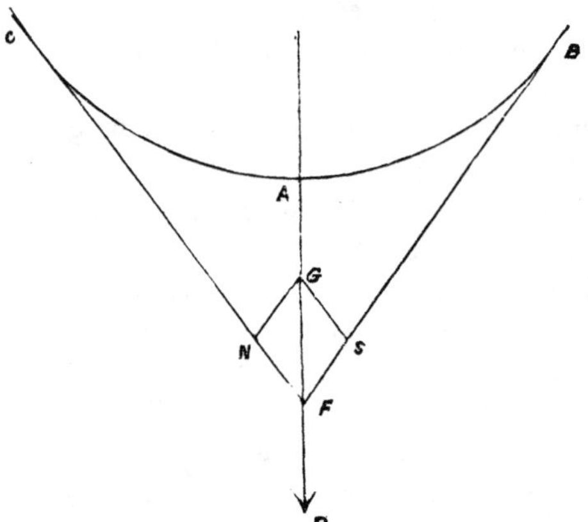

distributed over the cord, but we may find its resultant. Let P be this resultant and P F its direction. The *three* forces, viz.: the pulls at C and B, and the resultant of the load, P, are all in the same vertical plane; they are the only forces acting on the cord; and as they are in equilibrium, the *directions of these three forces must meet in one point*, and the forces themselves *must be proportional to the three sides of a triangle drawn parallel to their directions.*

G N F (Fig. 1) is such a triangle. The known directions of the pulls at B and C, and of P, give us the angles in this triangle; and if we know also the magnitude of the load P, represented by the line G F, we can determine that of the pulls at B and C. For

(Pull at B =G N) : G F : : sin G F N : sin GNF.
(Pull at C=N F) . G F : : sin N G F : sin G N F.

The analysis we have made for the whole cord may be applied to any part of it. Thus, if we consider any arc B′ A′ (Fig. 2) of the cord, and the load on that arc, we have three forces in the same plane in equilibrium. For at A′ and B′ the other parts of the cord may be replaced by two hooks, and the pulls on these hooks, exerted by the cord at A′ and B′, will be, as before, in the direction of the tangents at those points. The resultant P′ of the load on A′ B′ must pass through the point of intersection of the tangents, and if the direction of that resultant be as indicated in the figure, then G′ N′ F′ will be the triangle of forces.

FIG. 2.

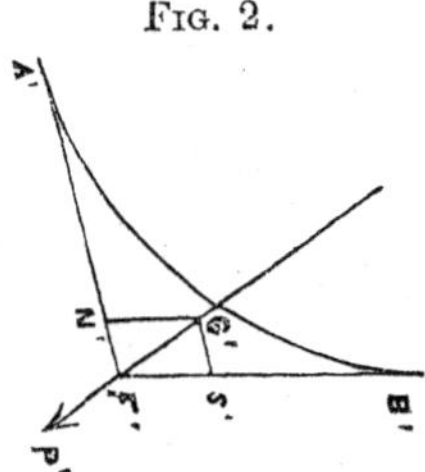

The principles above explained enable us to calculate the "pulls" at all points of a loaded chain or cord, and consequently to fix *its size and strength to bear* a given load; or to determine the *amount, distribution, and direction of the load* necessary to produce assumed "pulls" in a cord of a given shape.

Thus suppose in the half of the loaded cord of (Fig. 1) we draw the tangents at A and B (as is done in Fig. 3), the resultant of the load P *must* pass through F, the point of intersection of the tangents. If the direction and amount of P be known, lay off

Fig. 3.

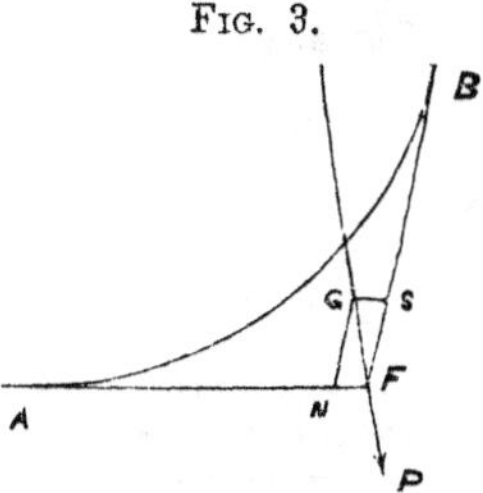

F G to represent it. Then, as above explained,

N F = pull at A

and

N G = pull at B.

Suppose, on the other hand, we assume the pulls at A and B to be equal, we lay off on the two tangents (Fig. 4), equal lengths, F S and F N, to represent these equal pulls, and upon them construct a parallelogram. Then F G gives the magnitude and direction of the resultant of the load that must be put on the cord to produce the given pulls.

A cord is in *equilibrium* when it is balanced under the load applied. Change the distribution of the load and the cord

Fig. 4.

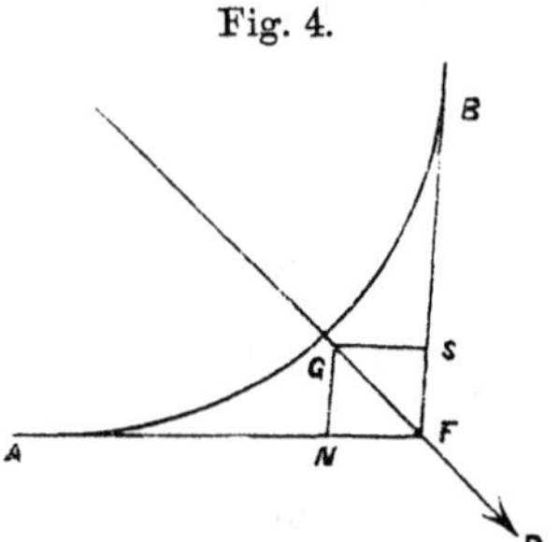

at once changes shape and assumes the form necessary to equilibrium under the new load.

Thus, if P (Fig. 5) equals the direction of the resultant of the new load on the cord from the horizontal point A to the point of support B, draw the tangent A F, until it meets the direction of the load P, at F; then draw F B. The cord A B will have so changed its form that F B (Fig. 5) will now be the direction of the tangent at B.

FORMS OF CORDS UNDER VARIOUS LOADS.

Let us now investigate the various curves which a cord will assume under different distributions of the load.

FIG. 5.

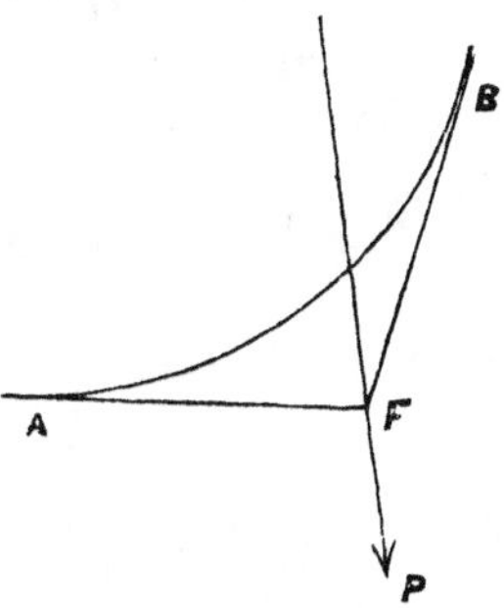

Case I. Suppose the load to be altogether *vertical*, and to be distributed *uniformly* along the *horizontal*.

Let *equal* weights be hung, for instance, along a cord C B (Fig. 6) so that the *horizontal* distance between the threads by which the weights are suspended shall be everywhere equal. Or, draw little elementary triangles along the curve, so that the *bases* of all these little triangles shall be equal, and let the threads holding the weights cut the middle of these bases. Then each weight may be considered as the resultant of the load on the element of the curve which constitutes the hypothenuse of the little triangle to which it is attached. Such a load is *vertical* and is *uniformly distributed along the horizontal.*

Fig. 6.

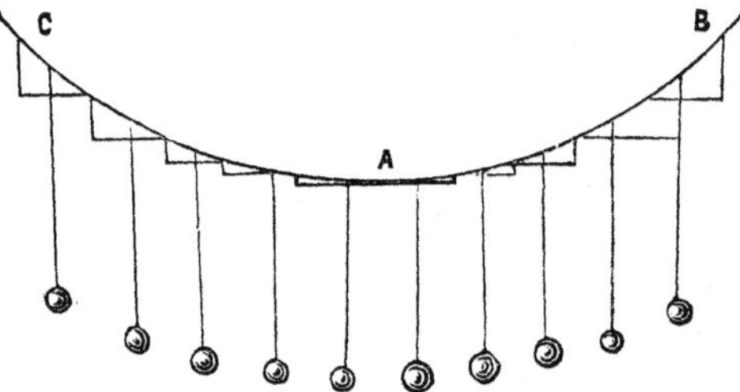

To determine the curve of the cord. Obtain the resultant of the load between the horizontal point A and the point B (Fig. 7). This resultant, as the little forces are all parallel, is equal to the sum of them, and it is vertical in direction. It will also evidently bisect A T. Draw it, and from its point of intersection with A T, draw the line F B, which, as has been shown, must be tangent at B. Prolong B F to I, then the subtangent I J is seen to be bisected at the vertex A of the curve. Hence the curve C B is a *parabola*.

FIG. 7.

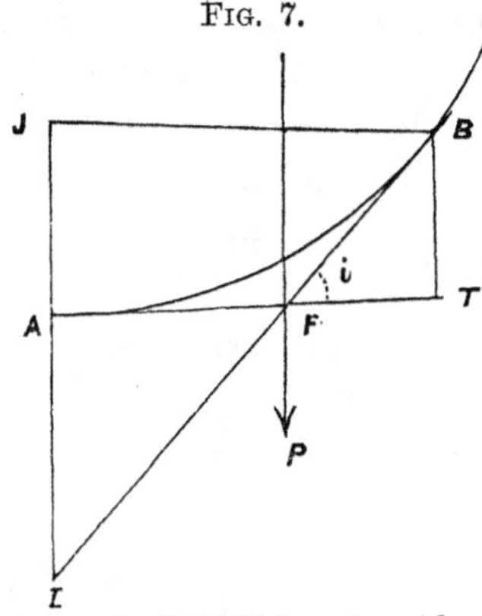

The triangle B F T has its sides parallel to the forces acting on the half cord A B; so that if B T be taken to represent P,

B F = pull at B
F T = pull at A.

Let T = equal tension at any point along the cord.
H = value of T at the horizontal point A, or the "horizontal pull" on the cord.
i = inclination of the tangent at any point to the horizontal.

Then as the arc A F (Fig. 7) may stand for any part of the curve counting from the horizontal point A towards one of the points of suspension, we have the following general equations from the triangle B F T:

$$T^2 = P^2 + H^2 \qquad (1.)$$

$$\text{Tan } i = \frac{P}{H} = \frac{p x}{H} = \frac{d y}{d x} \qquad (2.)$$

(p being = the load per unit of horizontal distance, A the origin of co-ordinates, A T = axis of X and A J = axis of y).

From equations (1) and (2) we can solve three problems.

1. Given the *curve*, and the *load*, to find T and H.

2. Given the *curve*, and T and H, to find P.

3. Given the *load*, and T and H, to find the curve.

For a full discussion of this case, see Rankine's "Civil Engineering."

Such a distribution of the load as we have discussed in the above case, is approximated to in suspension bridges, and sometimes in wood, iron, or steel arches, but not usually in stone or brick ones.

FIG. 8.

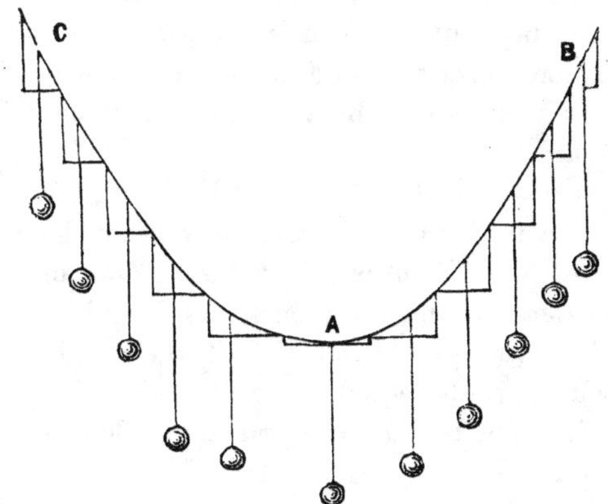

Case II. Let the load still be *vertical*, but distributed *uniformly along the curve.*

That is, divide the arc C A B (Fig. 8) into elements each of a unit in length; then the load on these elements is constant throughout. It is easily seen that such a load is not, as in the last case, uniform along the *horizontal*, for the *bases* of the little triangles of which the *hypothenuses* are now equal, diminish in extent as we go from A towards B or C. A chain of uniform material and cross-section and acted on by nothing but its own weight, is in the condition described, and, as is well known, the curve assumed by it is the "common catenary."

Let p = weight of a unit's length of the cord, then if $p\ m$ = horizontal pull on the cord at A = H, m is called the *modulus* of the *catenary*, and represents the length of cord of the same kind as C B, the weight of which would equal the pull at A. The weight on A B = P = $p\ s$ when s = length of cord A B.

The triangle of forces for any arc A D (Fig. 9) can be found as before, by drawing the tangents at A and D, and the line representing the force P vertically through their intersections. The triangle D F T will represent the forces; D T being = P

$= p\,s$, and F T $=$ H $= p\,m$, and D F $=$ T $=$ tension at D. Then

FIG. 9.

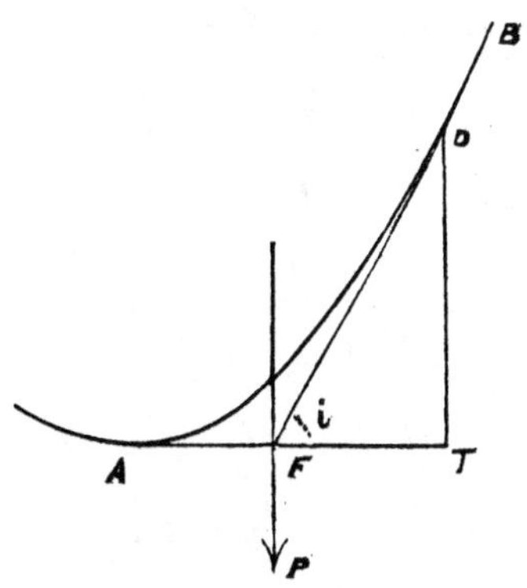

$$T^2 = H^2 + P^2 = p^2\,m^2 + p^2\,s^2 = p^2\,(s^2 + m^2) \quad (3.)$$

$$\text{Tan } i = \frac{D\,T}{F\,T} = \frac{p\,s}{p\,m} = \frac{s}{m} = \frac{d\,y}{d\,x} \quad (4.)$$

From the differential equation

$$\frac{d\,y}{d\,x} = \frac{s}{m}$$

we obtain the linear equation of the curve. In doing so it is most convenient to take the origin at a point O, whose distance below the vertex A is $= m$. The line Q O X

(Fig. 10) is called the *directrix* of the catenary.

The equations of the catenary are

$$s = \frac{m}{2}\left\{ E^{\frac{x}{m}} - E^{-\frac{x}{m}} \right\} = \sqrt{y^2 + m^2} = \text{length* of arc.} \qquad (5.)$$

$$y = \frac{m}{2}\left\{ E^{\frac{x}{m}} + E^{-\frac{x}{m}} \right\} = \sqrt{s^2 + m^2} \qquad (6.)$$

$$x = m.\ \text{hy. log.} \left\{ \frac{1}{\frac{y}{m} + \sqrt{\frac{y^2}{m^2} - 1}} \right\} \qquad (7.)$$

$$\text{Area A O E D} = \int y\,dx = m\,s \qquad (8.)$$

$$\text{Tan } i = \frac{s}{m} = \tfrac{1}{2}\left\{ E^{\frac{x}{m}} - E^{-\frac{x}{m}} \right\} \qquad (9.$$

$$\text{Radius of curv.} = \rho = \frac{y^2}{m^2} = \frac{m^2 + s^2}{m} \qquad (10.)$$

Since the area A O E D $= m\ s$, and m = a constant, the area varies as s. But the load on the arc A D ($= p\,s$) also varies as s, since p is constant. Hence a convenient mode of representing the load on any arc, A D. Suppose a sheet of metal C Q T B A C (Fig. 10), bounded below by the "directrix," Q T, to be suspended from the curve. Let

---

* E = Base of Naperian Logarithms.

the weight of this metal corresponding to m units of its surface be $= p$. That is, let

$$w\,m = p, \text{ or } w = \frac{p}{m}.$$

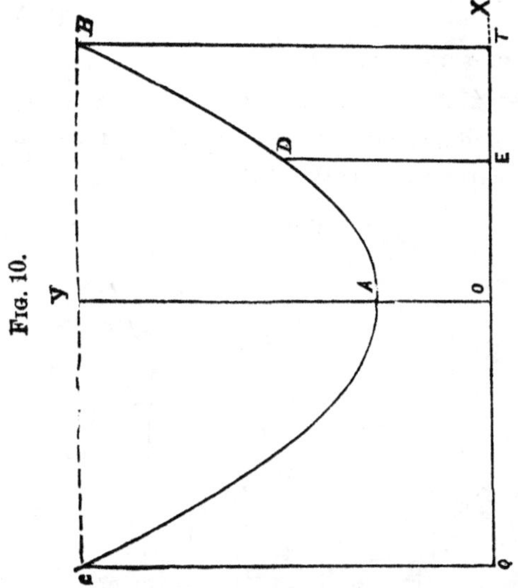

Fig. 10.

The weight of a strip a *unit in breadth* extending from A to O is then $= p =$ the weight of a unit's length of the cord. Then the part of the sheet A O D E whose weight $= w\,m\,s = p\,s$, represents the weight P on the arc A D. So A O B T represents the weight on A B, and C Q T B the whole weight on C A B. In the horizontal pull at A we have

$$H = p\,m = w\,m^2 \qquad (11.)$$

and at any point D

$$T = \sqrt{H^2 + P^2} = p\sqrt{s^2 + m^2} = p\,y = w\,m\,y. \qquad (12.)$$

The property above explained may be illustrated in another way.

FIG. 11.

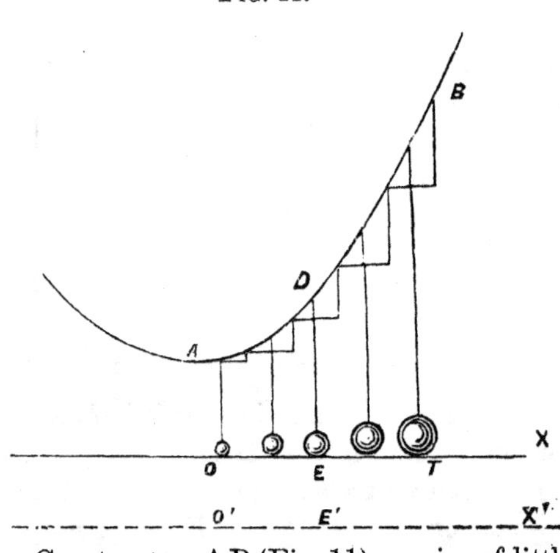

Construct on AB (Fig. 11) a series of little

triangles with all their *bases* equal. Let the weights of the little arcs constituting the hypothenuses of these triangles be represented by balls suspended by threads from the middle of each little arc. Take the length of the thread corresponding to the ball at A as $= m$; make the lengths of all the threads proportional to the weights of the balls hung to them; then the lower ends of these lines will all be on the directrix O X. That is, the *intensity* of the load on a catenary along the horizontal line (= weight on a unit of horizontal distance) varies as the *ordinates* of the catenary, when those ordinates are measured from the directrix.

It makes no difference in the form of the curve A B (Fig. 11), to increase or diminish the weights provided the *proportion* among them is preserved. Thus we may assume the cord and the sheet C Q T B (Fig 10), to be of a different material in which a unit's length of the cord shall in weight $= p'$, and the weight of the sheet per unit of surface shall $= w'$, and A B will be unchanged. Note, however, that we cannot change the depth A O of the sheet (Fig. 10), nor the length of the lines (Fig. 11), without changing the curve, for if the lines ended in O′ X′ for instance, instead of O X, then $\frac{A\,O}{D\,E}$ would *not* be equal to $\frac{A\,O'}{D\,E'}$

Hence, the *modulus* (m = A O) fixes the catenary, or if we assume the catenary, this determines the modulus. Thus if we assume three points, B, A, C (Fig. 10), on the catenary the distance A O is thereby determined; and if we assume A O' and the point A we cannot generally assume B and C.

This often interferes with the use of the "common catenary" in the building of arches [in which case the curve is inverted, the metal sheet A O T D is replaced by a wall of uniform material, and the tension on its cord, C B (Fig. 10), is replaced by a thrust along C A B (Fig. 12)]. For we are often compelled to make the curve pass through three points, while yet the value of A O is fixed.

But this difficulty may be obviated by the

use of the *transformed catenary*, which we will now discuss.

FIG. 12.

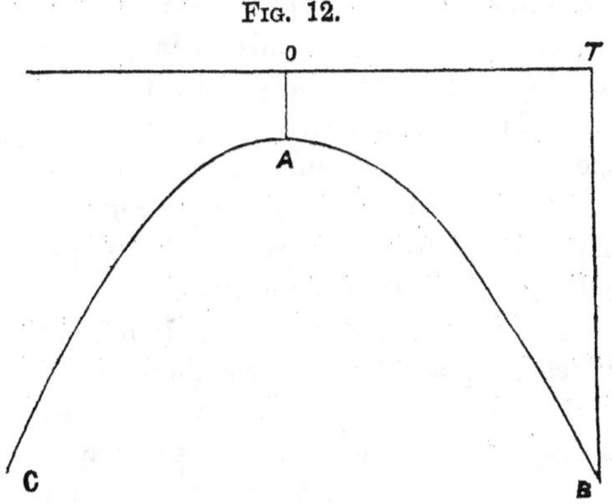

Case III. By the principle of *Parallel Projections*, if any cord or arched rib is balanced under a system of forces which are represented in the figure by lines, and a *parallel projection* be made of the curve of the cord or rib and of the lines representing the forces, then the new curve will represent a cord or rib that will be balanced under the forces represented by the new lines.

Imagine a cylindrical surface constructed upon C Q T B A C (Fig. 10) as a base. To simplify matters, suppose the elements of the cylinder to be perpendicular to the plane of the base. Cut this cylinder by a plane inclined to the base, and we shall get a "Transformed Catenary," and the shape of the sheet of metal under which it will be balanced; for the new curve and surface cut out by the inclined plane are the *parallel projections* of the curve C A B and the surface C Q T B A C (Fig. 10). Let this inclined plane be so placed that it shall intersect the plane of the base in the straight line C B (Fig. 10) or in one parallel to it. Then all horizontal lines (or those parallel to C B or Q T) will be unchanged in length in the parallel projection, while all vertical lines (those parallel to A O, etc.) will be lengthened in a constant ratio whose magnitude will depend upon the inclination of the cutting plane. Make a vertical section of the cylinder on the line OY. Then if the cutting plane passes though C B we get the triangle O U Y (Fig. 13*a*) cut out of the wedge to which the cylinder reduces in this case. In the triangle, U V is the ordinate of the vertex of the *transformed catenary* corresponding to O A in

FIG 13 (*a*).

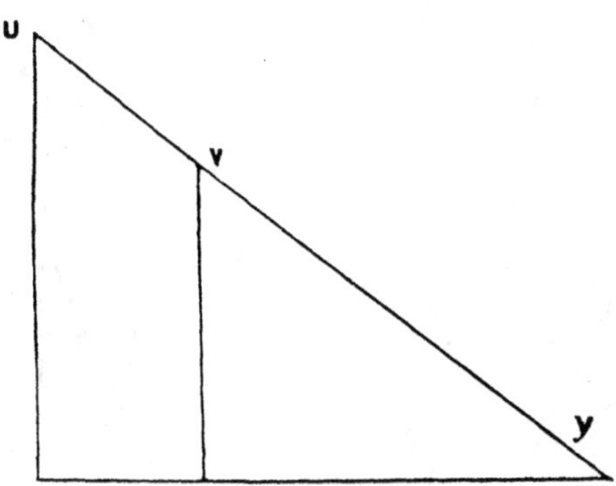

the *common catenary*, and all lines parallel to U V are evidently increased over the corresponding ones of which they are the parallel projections, in the same ratio that U V exceeds O A. Laid down in the same plane the two curves are C A B and C′ A′ B′ (Fig. 13 *b*).

It is easy to pass from a given catenary to a transformed catenary whose ordinates shall be *shorter* instead of *longer* than those of the given curve, by erecting an oblique cylinder on the given catenary and surface C Q T B, and cutting it by a plane

Fig. 13 (*b*).

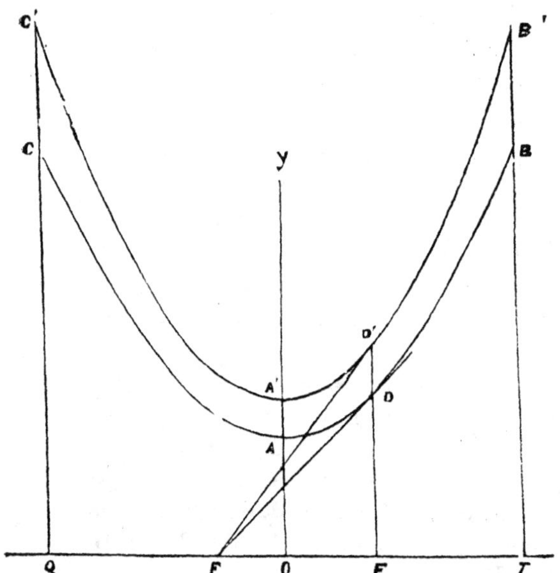

less oblique than the base. So too, the horizontal dimensions can be changed instead of the vertical, by making the cutting plane meet the base in a line parallel to O Y, instead of in one parallel to Q T.

The equations of the curve C′ A′ B′ (Fig. 13 *b*,) are thus obtained. The *abscissas* are the same as those in C A B, but the ordinates are changed, so that (if y' = general ordinate of C′ A′ B′ and y_o = A′ O, the ordinate at the vertex A′)

$$y' : y :: A'O : AO :: y_o : m.$$

$$\therefore y' = \frac{y_0}{m} \cdot y \text{ or } y = y' \frac{m}{y_0}$$

In the equations of the common catenary substitute y' for y and we have the equations of C′ A′ B′.

From equation (6)

$$\frac{m}{y_0} \cdot y' = \frac{m}{2} \left\{ E^{\frac{x}{m}} + E^{-\frac{x}{m}} \right\}$$

$$\therefore y' = \frac{y_0}{2} \left\{ E^{\frac{x}{m}} + E^{-\frac{x}{m}} \right\} \qquad (13.)$$

So equation (7) becomes

$$x = m \text{ hy. log.} \left\{ \frac{1}{\frac{y'}{y_0} + \sqrt{\frac{y'^2}{y_0^2} - 1}} \right\} \qquad (14.)$$

So equation (8) or area A′ O E D′.

$$= \int y' . d\,x = \frac{m\,y_0}{2} \left\{ E^{\frac{x}{m}} - E^{-\frac{x}{m}} \right\} \qquad (15.)$$

etc., etc., etc.

The "triangle of forces" F E D (Fig. 13 *b*), for any arc A D of the catenary, becomes F E D′ for the arc A′ D′ of the transformed catenary—that is, since the horizontal lines and forces are unchanged.

Tension at vertex A′ = H′ = H = wm^2 16.)

Load on A′ D′ is increased in ratio of A′ O to A O or of D′ E to D E.

$$\therefore P' = P.\frac{D'E}{DE} = P.\frac{y_0}{m} \quad (17.)$$

(D′ E represents this load.)

Then tension at D′ is

$$T' = \sqrt{P'^2 + H^2} \quad (18.)$$

and

$$\text{Tan } i = \frac{dy'}{dx} = \frac{y_0}{2m}\left\{E^{\frac{x}{m}} - E^{-\frac{x}{m}}\right\} \quad (19.)$$

In this curve we can assume the directrix Q T, the distance A′ O (= y_0) and also the points B′ and C′. These quantities assumed, we determine m (the modulus of the corresponding common catenary) from equation (14), and then by equation (13) find points of the transformed catenary.

From equations (18) and (19) we can solve three problems similar to those given under the head of Case I.

Case IV. So far we have discussed the forms of cords under loads *parallel* and altogether *vertical.* Let us take up the cases of loads varying in direction.

Suppose (as Case IV.) that the load be *uniform* and *normal* at *every point* to the cord. Such a load is represented in (Fig. 14), the load on each element $d\ s$ of the curve being constant and perpendicular to it.

FIG. 14.

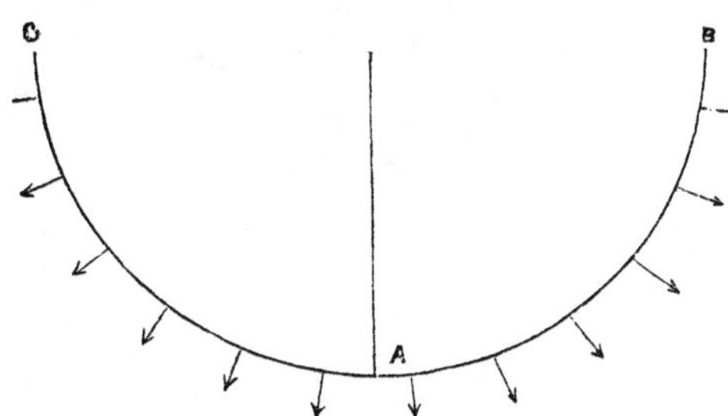

It is first to be noted that the pull or tension on a cord under *any* load which is *everywhere normal* to it, must be *constant.* That is, the pull along the cord at A and B, and at all other points, is one and the same. That the tension at B in the cases previously discussed is greater than at A, is due to the fact that the elements of the load between A and B have in those cases *tangential* components, which go to change the value of the pull along the cord. But in the present case, the load being *everywhere* normal, there are no such tangential components, and therefore the "pull" does not change.

FIG. 15.

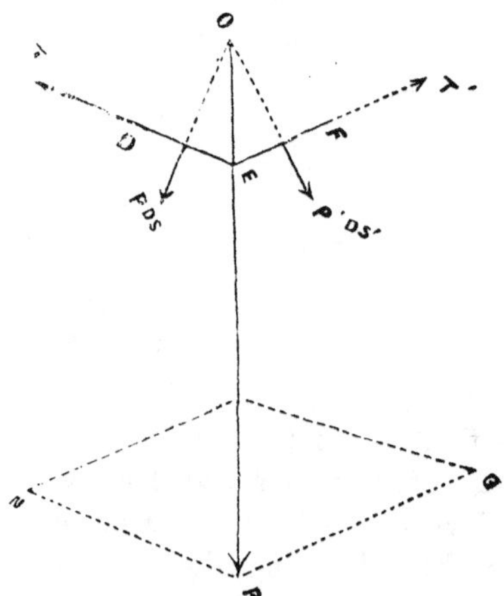

Take any two adjoining elements of the

cord $d\,s$ (= D E, Fig. 15) and $d\,s'$ (= E F, Fig. 15), each of such length as to correspond to equal elements of the load. The little loads on these lines we will represent by $p\ d\ s$, and $p'\ d\ s'$. Note, that unless the load be uniform all around the cord, $d\,s$ will not be equal to $d\,s'$. The equal loads $p\,d\,s$ and $p'\ d\ s'$ being normal respectively to D E and E F, their resultant which lies in the direction O R (Fig. 15) bisects the angle between $p\ d\ s$ and $p'\ d\ s'$, and also the angle D E F between $d\ s$ and $d\ s'$, which last is the angle between the direction of the pulls T and T′ on the cord at D F. Hence the parallelogram of forces (as shown at R) will be a rhombus, or

$$\text{N R} = \text{T} = \text{R G} = \text{T}'$$

Again, take *three* elements, D E, E F, F H (Fig. 16), of the cord, each bearing the normal load $p\ d\ s = p\ d\ s = p\ d\ s$. In place of the little arcs, we use for clearness the chords of those arcs. Since the load around the whole curve C A B (Fig. 14) is supposed to be *uniform*, the arcs bearing the equal elements ($p\,d\,s$) of that load must also be equal, or D E = E F = F H. We have above proved T = T′. Hence the three sides D E, E F, and F H will arrange themselves symmetrically as in (Fig 16).

Fig. 16.

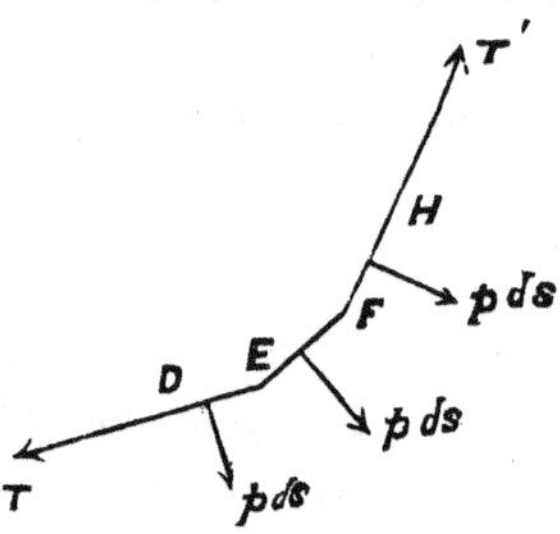

Now, every other piece of the cord containing three elements will assume exactly the same slope as D H, since each such piece must equal D H in length and must be acted on by an equal and precisely similar system of forces. Consequently, the little chords D E, etc., must constitute a *regular polygon*, and the curve in which they are inscribed must be *constant* in curvature, in other words—a *circle*.

Therefore the curve of the cord C A B (Fig. 14) is the arc of a circle.

To form the triangle of forces for any point of a loaded circle as for A D (Fig. 17),

FIG. 17.

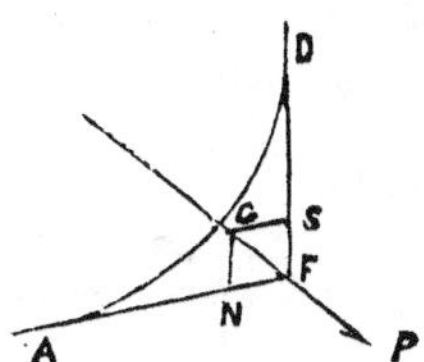

draw the tangents at the extremities A and D. From the intersection, F, of these, lay off F N = F S, to represent the equal pulls at A and D. Then the diagonal F G=the resultant of the load, and the triangle F N G or F S G represents the forces acting on A D.

It is often easier to deal with a *uniform normal* load by resolving it into its vertical and horizontal components. The load on an element D E = ds of the quadrant A B (Fig. 18) is $= p\ d\ s$. The horizontal component of this load $= p d s$ sin. θ, where θ = the angle made by the direction of pds with the vertical (or what is the same, the angle made by the tangent of ds with the horizontal). The vertical component $= pds$ cos. θ. Consider the horizontal component (pds sin. θ) with reference to the vertical space over which it is distributed. This

FIG. 18.

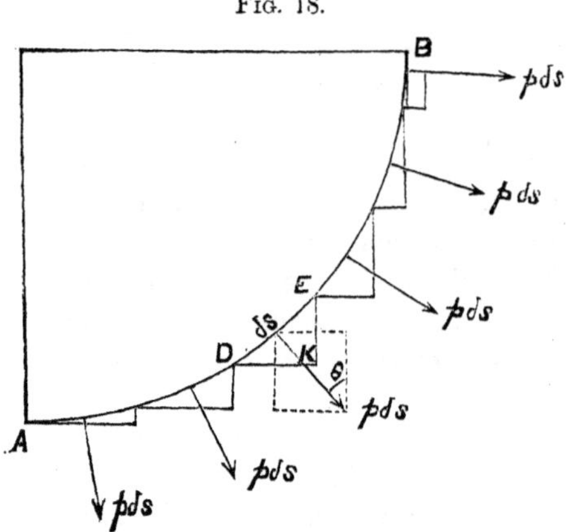

space is E K. (Fig. 18) $= d\,s$ sin. θ. Hence the *intensity* of the horizontal component

$$= \frac{p\;d\;s\;\sin\,\theta}{d\;s\;\sin\,\theta} = p.$$

So the vertical component ($p\;d\;s$ cos θ) is distributed over a horizontal space $=$ D K

$= d\,s \cos\theta$, and therefore its *intensity* is

$$= \frac{p\,d\,s \cos\theta}{d\,s \cos\theta} = p.$$

But $p =$ the *intensity* of the normal force. Hence the original normal force at each point is equivalent to a horizontal and a vertical force, at that point, of equal intensity.

If we then construct little triangles on the curve A B (Fig. 19) such that their

FIG. 19.

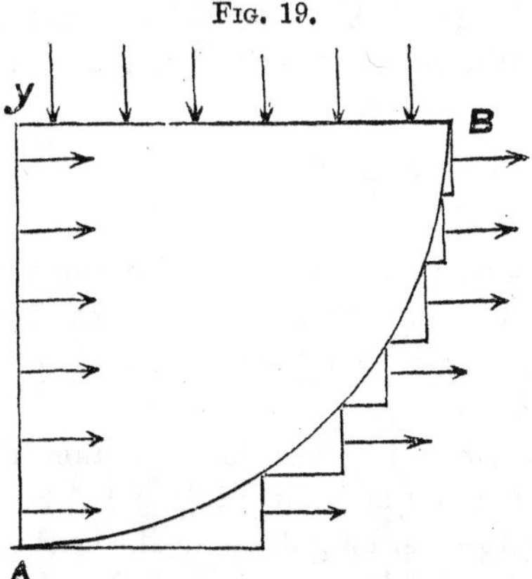

vertical sides shall be constant in length,

the horizontal forces on these sides will be represented by lines of constant length. Transfer these forces in their lines of direction to A Y. A Y is the sum of all the vertical sides of the little triangles, and as the horizontal *intensity* is constant and equal to p, we have (if $r =$ radius of the circle) p (A Y) $= pr =$ total horizontal force on quadrant A B.

Similarly, if we draw a set of triangles on A B with all their *horizontal* sides of the same length, we may see that the total vertical force on A B is

$$= p \,.\, (\text{Y B}) = p\,r.$$

Hence,

1. The resultant of the entire normal force on the quadrant A B is equal to the resultant of a horizontal and a vertical force each of which is $= pr$.

2. Therefore in the parallelogram of forces for the quadrant (Fig. 20), F S, which represents the pull along the cord at B, is the vertical component of P, while N F = pull at A, is the horizontal component of P. Each of these forces $= pr$.

Therefore the constant pull all along the cord is $= pr$.

If we make the pull at the vertical point (B) $=$ V, we have

$$H = V = T = p\,r \quad . \quad . \qquad (20.)$$

In practice a uniform normal force exists in the case of a cylinder filled with steam, or in a vertical cylinder filled with liquid.

FIG. 20.

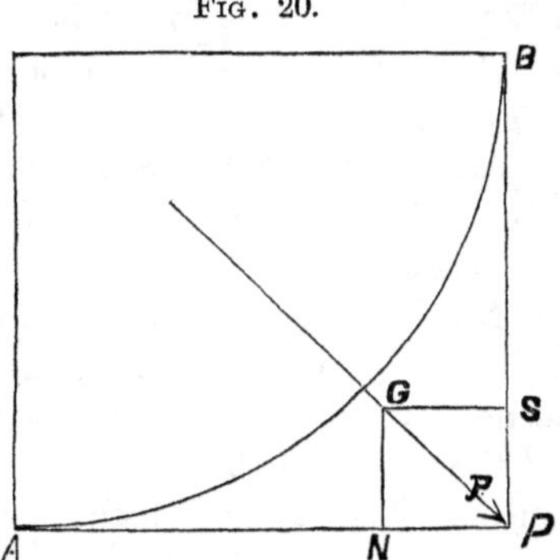

Thrust instead of tension along A B exists when the normal force pushes inwards, as in the tubes of a steam boiler or an empty vertical cylinder immersed in water. In reference to arches, this discussion has its principal value as introductory to those that follow.

Case V. In this case we obtain the curve and forces by parallel projections from the circle.

If we suppose a cylinder erected upon the circle (Fig. 21) as a base and cut it by an inclined plane whose line of intersection with the plane of the base shall be parallel to A I, we will get an ellipse whose vertical axis A′ I′ (Fig. 21) will = A I, and whose horizontal axis C′ B′ will be greater than C B. All lines parallel to A I will be unchanged in length, while all parallel to C B will be increased in the proportion of C′ B′ to C B. Now, by the principle of parallel projections, the ellipse, which is the parallel projection of the circle, will be balanced under the forces which are the parallel projections of those under which the circle is balanced.

As we have seen, the circle is the curve assumed by the ring under a uniform horizontal and vertical force at each point of the same kind, and equal in intensity; for such

Fig. 21.

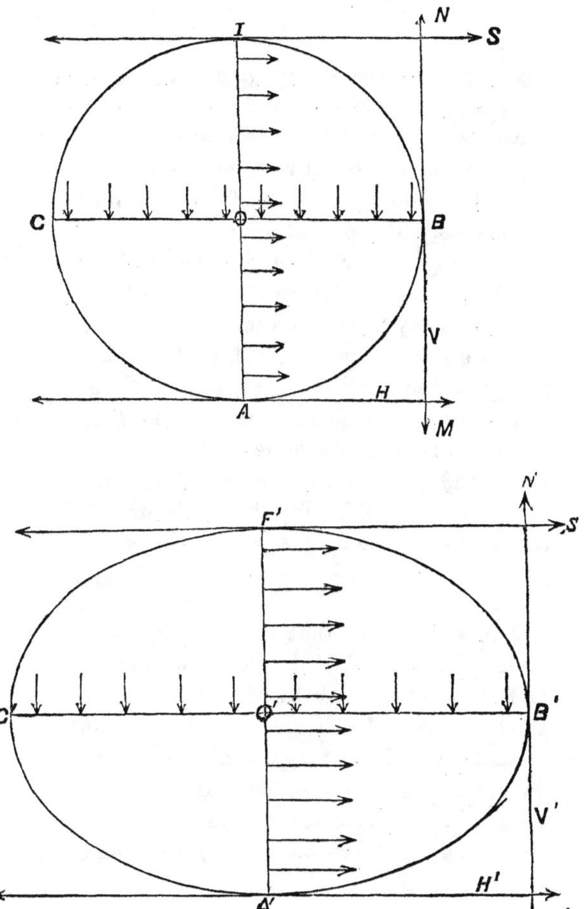

a system of forces is equivalent to a constant normal force around the curve. For convenience, these forces are represented in Fig. (21) along the two diameters, each little line representing the force on a unit of distance. The pull around the ring is of course tangential to it, and is everywhere the same ($= pr$). This pull is represented at A and B by the arrows there.

In the ellipse, the *vertical* lines being unchanged, the total vertical force on the elliptic ring ($=$ the sum of all the little vertical lines) is the same as it was in the circle, and if we call the vertical force on a quadrant V ($=$ B M) for the circle and V′ ($=$ B′ M′) for the ellipse, we will have

$$V = V' \quad . \quad . \quad . \quad (21.)$$

Notice, however, that in the ellipse the force V′ is distributed over the distance O′ B′ and not over a distance $=$ O B. Hence the *intensity* of the force V′, or the amount of that force on each unit of distance, is not the same as in the circle. In the ellipse (Fig. 21) each little vertical line represents, therefore, the force on a distance greater than a unit. Let $O'B' = c\,OB$. Then to obtain the *intensity* of V′, divide it by the space over which it is distributed. Thus, let

$$p_y = \frac{V}{OB} \text{ and } p_x = \frac{H}{AO}$$

represent the vertical and horizontal intensities in the circle. We have already seen that in the circle

$$p_y = p_x = p.$$

Let p'_y and p'_x represent the vertical and horizontal intensities in the ellipse. Then

$$p'_y = \frac{V'}{O'B'} = \frac{V}{c.OB} = \frac{p_y}{c} \qquad (22.)$$

The lines representing the "pulls" at B and C (as B N) are also unchanged. Hence the pulls at those points in the elliptic ring are the same as in the circular; that is they are equal to $V' = V$.

The *horizontal* lines are all increased in length in the ratio $1 : c$. Hence the sum of the lines representing the horizontal force on a quadrant of the ellipse (as I′ S′) is greater than the corresponding line (I S) in the circle in the above ratio. Therefore if

$H' =$ the horizontal force on the elliptical quadrant,

$$H' = c \cdot H \quad . \quad . \quad (23.)$$

The length over which this force H' is distributed $(A'\,O')$ does not change, however, and hence the little horizontal lines in both figures represent the force on a unit of distance. Hence the *intensity* of the horizontal force in the ellipse has increased just as the length of the lines, or from the equation

$$p'_x = \frac{H'}{A'\,O'} = \frac{c.H}{A\,O} = c\,p_x \quad (24.)$$

The horizontal pull in the ring at A' or I' being equal to the horizontal force on a quadrant is

$$H' = c.H = c.V = c.V' \quad . \quad . \quad (25.)$$

Hence the "pull" around the ellipse is *not* constant as it was in the circle. The pulls at B' and A' are as

$$V' : H' : : 1 : c.$$

But

$$A'\,I' : C'\,B' : : 1 : c.$$

Therefore,

1. The pulls in an elliptical ring are as the axes to which they are parallel.

Again the intensities in the ellipse are

$$p'_y : p'_x : : \frac{p_y}{c} : c\, p_x : : \frac{1}{c} : c : : 1 : c^2$$

And

$$(A' I')^2 : (C' B')^2 : : 1 : c^2$$

Therefore,

2. The *intensities* of the forces in an ellipse are as the *squares* of the axes to which they are parallel.

From this proportion we have

$$c = \sqrt{\frac{p'_x}{p'_y}} \quad . \quad . \quad . \quad (26.)$$

It will be noted in the elliptic ring that the resultant of the little horizontal and vertical loads at any point is not *normal* to the curve except at the extremities of the axes.

Let us determine the pulls and the relations between the forces at other points besides the extremities of the vertical and horizontal axes of the ellipse.

In the circle (Fig. 22) if we resolve the forces along any two rectangular axes as $A_1 I_1$ and $C_1 B_1$, we shall have evidently the same relations between them as when resolved along a vertical and horizontal axis.

Fig. 22.

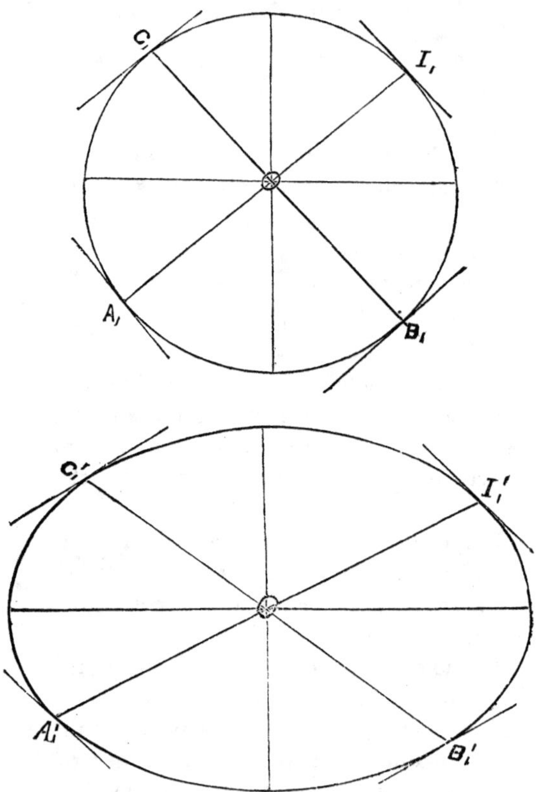

Now the three parallel lines, viz., the diameter, $A_1 I_1$, and the tangents at C_1 and B_1, are projected in the ellipse into three *parallel* lines, viz.: A'_1, I'_1, and the tangents at C'_1 and B'_1. Similarly C_1, B_1, and the tangents at A_1 and I_1 continue parallel in the ellipse. Hence *rectangular* diameters of the circle become *conjugate* in the ellipse. The lines representing the forces perpendicular to $C_1 B_1$ in the circle become parallel to $O' I'_1$ in the ellipse, and are changed in length just as $O' I'_1$ is changed from $O I_1$. So the forces which are parallel to $C_1 O$ in the circle become parallel to $C'_1 O'$ in the ellipse, and vary as $C'_1 O'$ does from $C_1 O$.

Let $O' I'_1 = r'$ and $O C'_1 = r''$ and let the total force parallel to $O' I'_1$ on a quadrant (such as $C'_1 I'_1$ or $I'_1 B'_1$) of the ellipse be $= V_1$ and that parallel to $O' B_1'$ be $= H_1$. Then if $r =$ radius of the circle, we have (since the force on a quadrant of the circle as $C_1 I_1$ is $= H = V = T$)

$$\left.\begin{array}{l} H : H_1 :: r : r'' \qquad \therefore H_1 = \dfrac{H . r''}{r} \\ V : V_1 :: r : r' \qquad \therefore V_1 = \dfrac{V\, r'}{r} = \dfrac{H . r'}{r} \\ \therefore H_1 : V_1 :: r'' : r' \end{array}\right\} \quad (27.)$$

H_1 is equal to the pull along the ring at A'_1 or I'_1, and V_1 is that at C'_1 and B'_1.

Hence *proposition* 1 may be applied generally to all conjugate diameters in the ellipse; that is,

3. The total pulls along the ring at the extremities of any two conjugate diameters, are as the diameters to which they are parallel.

Again, the *intensities* being equal to the total loads divided by the surfaces over which they are distributed, let

p'_{v_1} = intensity of load parallel to $O'\ I'_1$,
p'_{x_1} " " " $C'_1\ O'$

Then

$$\left.\begin{array}{l} p'_{v_1} = \dfrac{V_1}{O'C'_1} = \dfrac{V\,r'}{r\,.\,r''} = p_v\,\dfrac{r'}{r''} \\[2ex] p'_{x_1} = \dfrac{H_1}{O'I_1'} = \dfrac{H\,r''}{r\,.\,r''} = p_x\,\dfrac{r''}{r'} \\[2ex] \therefore p'_{v_1} : p'_{x_1} :: p_v\,\dfrac{r'}{r''} : p_x\,\dfrac{r''}{r'} :: \dfrac{r'}{r''} : \\[2ex] \qquad \dfrac{r''}{r'} :: r'^2 : r''^2 \end{array}\right\}(28.)$$

Hence for *proposition* 2, we may read,

4. The *intensities* of a pair of conjugate loads are to each other as the *squares* of the

conjugate diameters to which they are respectively parallel.

To pass from one set of conjugate forces on the ellipse to another ; let

p'_{x_1} and p'_{y_1} be the intensities parallel to one set of conjugate diameters.

H_1 and V_1 be total pulls parallel to same set of conjugate diameters.

r'' r' be the conjugate semidiameters.

Also let

$$p'_{1x_1},\ p'_{1y_1},\ H'_1,\ V'_1,\ r''_1,\ r'_1$$

be the corresponding quantities for the other set. Then

$$\left.\begin{array}{ll}
p'_{x_1} = p_x \dfrac{r''}{r'} & \therefore\ p_x = p'_{x_1} \dfrac{r'}{r''} \\
p'_{1x_1} = p_x \dfrac{r''_1}{r'_1} & \therefore\ p'_{1x_1} = p'_{x_1} \dfrac{r'\, r''_1}{r'_1\, r''} \\
\text{Also,} & \\
H_1 = \dfrac{H . r''}{r} & \text{or } H = \dfrac{H_1\, r}{r''} \\
H_1' = \dfrac{H\, r''_1}{r} & \therefore\ H'_1 = \dfrac{H_1\, r''_1}{r''} \\
\text{Similarly} & \\
p_1'_{y_1} = p'_{y_1} \dfrac{r''\, r'_1}{r'\, r''_1} & \\
V_1' = V_1 \dfrac{r'_1}{r'} &
\end{array}\right\} \quad (29)$$

The ellipse (Figs. 21 and 22) is the form assumed by a cord under a load composed of horizontal and vertical components which are constant along the horizontal and vertical lines, but which differ from each other in intensity.

The diameter C′ B′ of the ellipse (Fig. 21) might have been made *shorter* instead of *longer* than that of the circle, if required.

Cor.—If one set of the forces are vertical and the other not horizontal, but inclined at an angle to the horizon (Fig. 23), we still have an ellipse, the directions of the forces giving the directions of two conjugate diameters ($A'_1 O'$ and $B'_1 O'$). Then, if p'_{x_1} = the intensity of the inclined force and p'_{y_1} = intensity of the vertical force, we have by proposition 4,

$$p'_{x_1} : p'_{y_1} :: (B_1' O')^2 : (A_1' O')^2$$

So from proposition 3, if V_1 = pull along the cord at B_1' or C_1' and H_1 = that at A_1'

$$H_1 : V_1 :: B_1' O' : A_1' O'.$$

From the first of these propositions we have the ratio of the conjugate diameters;

and from the second we find the pulls at the extremities of those diameters.

Knowing two conjugate diameters and the angle ($90^{\circ}-j$) between them we can readily obtain the ellipse.

FIG. 23.

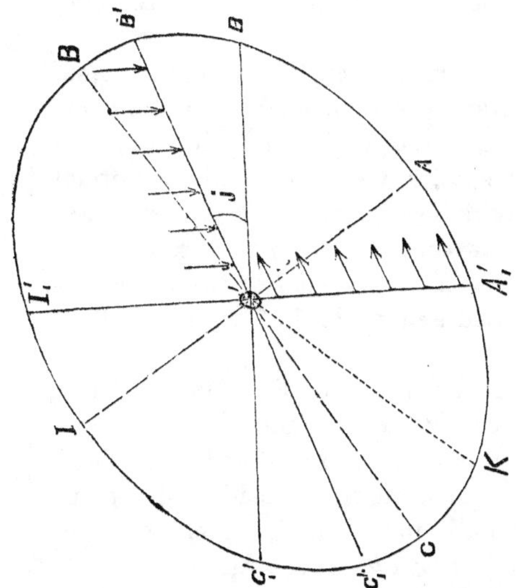

To obtain the pulls at the extremities of any diameter, such as $C_1 B_1$.

This is merely passing from one set of conjugate diameters to another and equation (29) gives the pull at B_1, for instance, as

$$V_1' = V_1 \frac{O' K}{O' A_1'}$$

($O' K$ being conjugate to $C_1 O' B_1$), etc., etc.

An important fact is now to be noted. Whenever the load on a cord is entirely *normal* to it, at that point the pull along the cord is equal to the intensity of the normal load multiplied by the radius of curvature.

For the cord *at that point* is similarly situated to a circular cord of the same curvature and under a load of the same intensity.

Thus, in the ellipse (Fig. 21) the action of the load at the extremities of the axes is entirely *normal*, for at A′ and I′ the horizontal component of the load vanishes and leaves only the vertical, which, *at these points*, is *normal* to the curve. So at C′ and B′ only the horizontal load has value, and its action is there normal to the curve.

Consider the elementary arc, ds, at A′,

for instance, which is subjected to this normal load. It is balanced under the equal pulls $T = T'$ (Fig. 24) coming from the adjoining parts of the cord, and the normal load *pds*, which gives it its curvature. Imagine a circle under a constant normal force of intensity $= p$. Take an equal little arc $d\,s$ of it, loaded with a normal load $=$ *pds.* Then, if it be acted on at its two ends by tensions $= T = T'$, it is evident that it will have the same curvature as the arc of the ellipse; or, conversely, if it has *the same curvature*, the pull around the circle *must* be $= T = T'$.

FIG. 24.

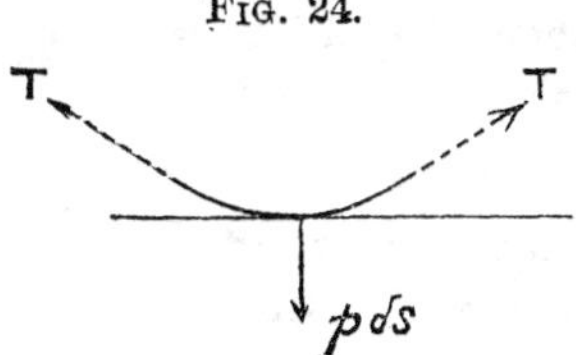

Hence, having given the load on the curve at any point where it is *normal*, we determine easily the pull along the cord at that point. For, in the circle,

$$H = V = T = p_x\ r = p_y\ r = p\ r$$

and in the ellipse at A′

$$H' = p'_y \rho$$

Where ρ = radius of curvature. If A′ O′ $= r$ and O′ B′ $= c\,r$ in the ellipse (Fig. 21) we have at A′

$$\rho = \frac{c^2 r^2}{r} = c^2 r.$$

$$\therefore H' = p'_y . c^2 r = \frac{p_y}{c} c^2 r = c\,p\,r = c\,H. \quad (30.)$$

So in the parabola under uniform vertical loads (Case I.) we have seen that H = $2\,p\,m$ (Rankine's C. E. p. 165). But H = $p\,\rho = 2\,p\,m$ (since $\rho = 2\,m$ at the vertex).

If the load be *everywhere* normal to the cord, the above equation will apply to every point, or

$$T = p\,\rho$$

be a general equation of the curve.

And further, when the load is everywhere normal we have already seen that the pull along the cord must be *constant*, as there is no tangential force to change it. Hence.

$$T = p\,\rho = \text{a constant.} \quad (31.)$$

When the load p is constant, of course, ρ

must be constant too, and we have the circle already discussed. When p varies, ρ must *vary inversely* as p.

Fig. 25.

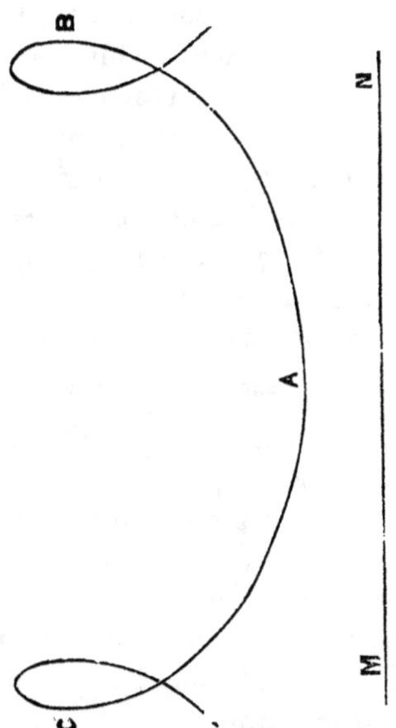

Case VI.—If p increases in value just in proportion to the distance of the points of the cord above a horizontal line M N (Fig.

25), the cord assumes the shape of the hydrostatic arch. This curve possesses geometrically the loops shown in the figure and may be extended indefinitely, but for our purpose it is evidently only necessary to discuss that part between the points C and B (Fig. 26) where the tangents are vertical.

Taking L (Fig. 26) for the origin, if the intensity of the load then be y_0 (= A L) multiplied by a constant, or wy_0, then at any other point it is $= wy$.

Hence the equation of the curve is

$$T = p\rho = wy\rho = wy_0\rho_0 = \text{a constant}$$

(y_0 and ρ_0 are the values of the ordinate and radius of curvature at A).

Let us resolve the normal load on C A B as we did in the circle, into its horizontal and vertical components. As was the case in the circle, these will be *for each point* equal in *intensity* to each other and also to the *normal* force, or

$$p = p_x = p_y.$$

But these quantities are no longer constant (as in the circle) all along the curve, but vary from point to point.

FIG. 26.

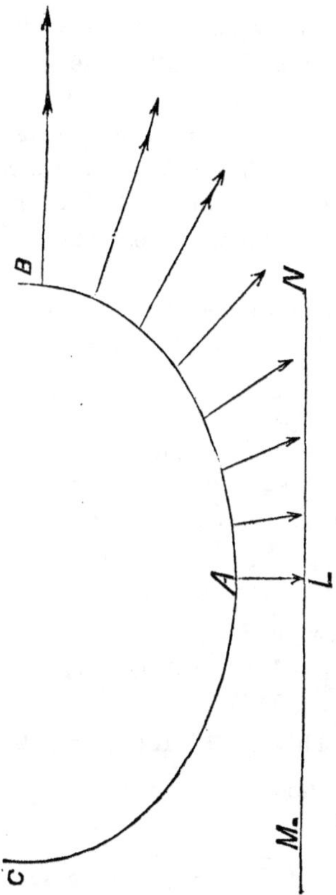

If we form the parallelogram of forces for any arc A D (as in Fig. 27) the side N F = F S, since H = T = a constant, and F G must represent the resultant of the whole load on A D both in amount and direction.

The vertical component, F E of F G, is equal to the vertical component S X of S F, or

Vertical load on A D = T sin i = H sin i.

At B the vertical load = T = H = V (since $i = 90°$ there).

So the horizontal component of the total load on A D is G E, and since

$$NF = GS = GE + FX$$

we have horizontal load on

$$AD = GE = NF - FX = H - H\cos i = H(1 - \cos i),$$

At B, $i = 90°$ ∴

Horizontal load on A B = H

On the arc D B

Horizontal load = H − H (1 − cos i) = H cos i.

The *vertical* load on A D may be thus expressed

$$H\sin i = \int_0^x p_y\,dx = w\int_0^x y\,dx = w\,y_0\,\rho_0 \sin i \quad (32.)$$

The *horizontal* load thus

$$H\,(1-\cos i)=w\,y_0\,\rho_0\,(1-\cos i)=\int_{y_0}^{y} p_x\,d\,y=$$

$$w\int_{y_0}^{y} y dy = w.\frac{y^2-y_0{}^2}{2} \qquad (33.)$$

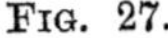

FIG. 27.

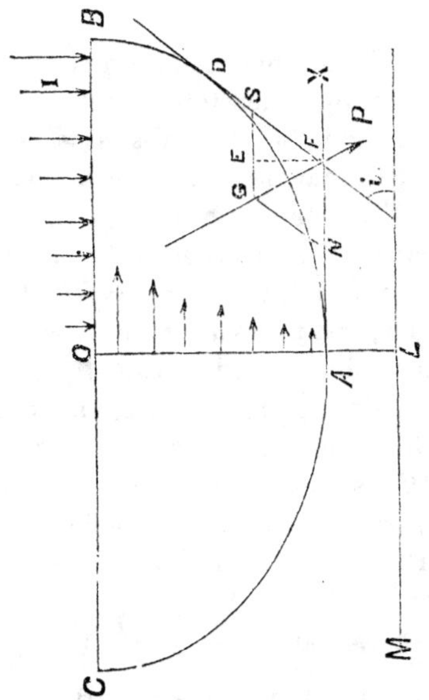

And if y_1 = ordinate of B, the horizontal load on A B is

$$H = w\frac{y_1^2 - y_0^2}{2} \qquad (34.)$$

For formula for radius of curvature see Rankine, C. E., p.

The equation $T = H = w\, y_0\, \rho_0 = w\, y\, \rho$, enables us to solve problems similar to those under the parabola.

Case VII.—If we construct a curve from the last one by using the same ordinates and by changing all the abscissas in the ratio $c : 1$, so that the new co-ordinates of a point shall be y and $c\,x$, and at the same time change the *horizontal* forces in the same proportion, leaving the *vertical* ones unchanged; the new curve and new system of forces so obtained will evidently be parallel projections of the former, and will be balanced. This new curve C′AB′ (Fig. 28) is the "Geostatic," and bears a relation to the "Hydrostatic" strictly analogous to that between the ellipse and circle.

Hence,

$$\left.\begin{array}{l}\text{The total vertical load on } A\,B' = V' = \\ \quad V = \text{pull along cord at } B'. \\ \text{Total horizontal load on } A\,B' = H' = \\ \quad c\,H = \text{pull along cord at } A'.\end{array}\right\} \quad (35.)$$

The *intensities* are

$$\left.\begin{array}{l} \text{For } \textit{vertical} \text{ load } p'_y = \dfrac{V'}{O\,B'} = \dfrac{V}{c.OB} = \dfrac{p_y}{c} \\ \text{For horizontal load } p'_x = \dfrac{H'}{O\,A} = \dfrac{c\,H}{O\,A} = c\,p_x \end{array}\right\} \quad (36.)$$

FIG. 28.

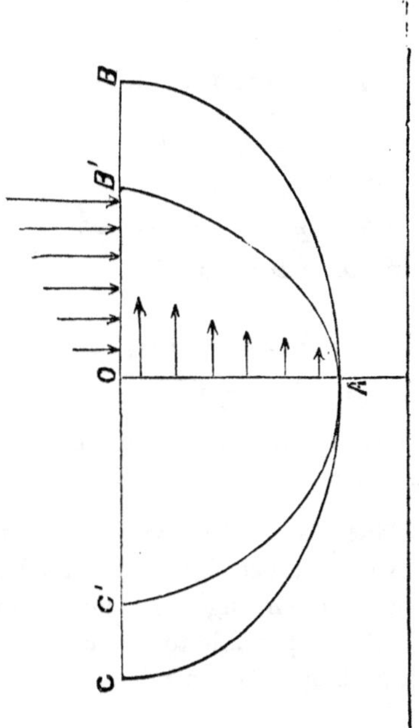

(V H p_x and p_y referring to the hydrostatic curve.)

The load at A and B′ and C′ being altogether *normal* (it is not so at the other points), let
ρ'_0 and ρ'_1 be the radii of curvature at A and B′.

Then

$$H' = p'_y \rho'_0 = \frac{p_y}{c} \rho'_0.$$

In the hydrostatic

$$H = p_y \rho_0. \quad \therefore c H = H' = c p_y \rho_0.$$

$$\therefore \frac{p_y}{c} \rho'_0 = c p_y \rho_0$$

$$\rho'_0 = c^2 \rho_0 \quad . \quad . \qquad (37.)$$

So

$$V' = p'_x \rho'_1 = c p_x \rho'_1 = V.$$

But in the hydrostatic

$$V = p_x \rho_1.$$

$$\therefore p_x \rho_1 = c p_x \rho'_1.$$

$$\therefore \rho'_1 = \frac{\rho_1}{c} \quad . \quad . \qquad (38.)$$

These radii are useful in drawing the geostatic curve.

Case VIII.—So far we have discussed the curves assumed by cords under loads distributed according to some simple law. But it is possible to discuss the more general problem: Given a load that varies and is distributed in any manner, required the curve which it will cause the cord to take; or conversely, given a curve, required the character and distribution of the load to produce it. The most useful form of the problem is that in which we assume the

FIG. 29.

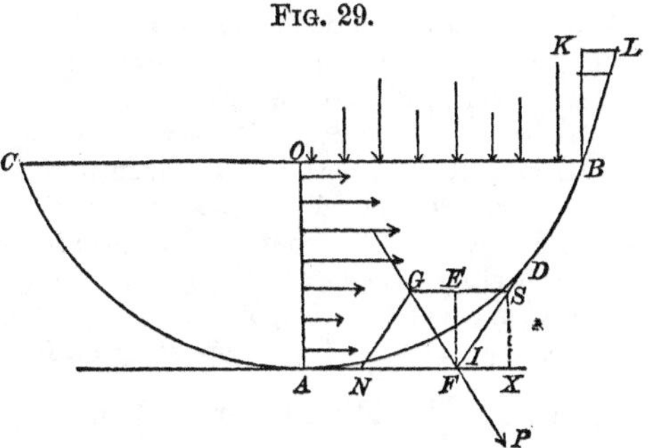

shape of the cord, and the *vertical components of the load*, and require to be found the intensity and distribution of the *horizontal components* of the load necessary to produce equilibrium.

To illustrate; assume the curve to be a circle, and the vertical load to be uniform in intensity, we see at once that the horizontal load should be also uniform, and of intensity equal to that of the vertical load.

But generally: Let C A B (Fig. 29) be some assumed curve, and let the vertical load be known in amount and distribution. Making some changes in the signification of the letters heretofore used, now let

V = vertical load on any arc A D.
V_1 = vertical load on the semi-cord A B.
H = horizontal load on any arc A D.
H_1 = " " half-cord A B.
H_0 = pull along cord at A (the quantity heretofore denoted by H).
p_x and p_y = the horizontal and vertical intensities as heretofore.
p_0 = value of p_y at the point A.
ρ_0 and ρ_1 = radii of curvature at A and B.

The vertical load on an arc A D is

$$V = \int_0^x p_y \, dx \quad . \quad . \quad (39.)$$

Again at the horizontal point A, the vertical projection of the element of the curve being = zero, the load is entirely vertical, and consequently at that point is *normal* to the curve. Hence the pull along the cord at A is

$$H_0 = p_0 \rho_0.$$

To discuss the forces upon an arc A D. Draw tangents at A and D. They meet at F (Fig. 29), through which point the resultant of the total load on A D must pass. The *vertical load* is also = the vertical component of the pull along the cord at D, for these two forces, being the only vertical ones connected with A D, must needs balance each other. Therefore,

Lay off F N $= H_0$. Lay off F E vertical and $= \int_0^x p_y \, dx$. Complete the rectangle F E S X. The pull along the cord at

$$D = F S = F E \operatorname{cosec} i = V \operatorname{cosec} i \quad . \quad . \quad (40)$$

Also,

$$S E = F X = V \cot i = \text{horizontal compound of pull along the cord at D} \quad . \quad . \quad (41)$$

But the horizontal pull at A is

$$H_0 = F N = G S.$$

$$\therefore G E = H_0 - V \cot i = H = \text{resultant of horizontal load on A D} \quad . \quad . \quad (42.)$$

The *intensity* of this horizontal load may be expressed thus

$$p_x = \frac{d H}{d y} = -\frac{\delta (V \cot i)}{d y} = -\frac{\delta \left(V \frac{d x}{d y} \right)}{d y} \quad (43.)$$

At B the vertical load $= V_1$. Let this be represented by B K (Fig. 29). If the cord be itself vertical at that point, B K $= V_1$ will be equal to the pull along it at B. If the cord is inclined as in the figure, draw its tangent at B, and

B L $=$ B K cosec $i_1 = V_1$ cosec $i_1 =$ pull along the cord.

and

K L $=$ B K cot $i_1 = V_1$ cot $i_1 =$ horizontal component of this pull.

$H_0 - V_1 \cot i_1 = H_1 =$ resultant of entire horizontal load on A B.

Fig. 30.

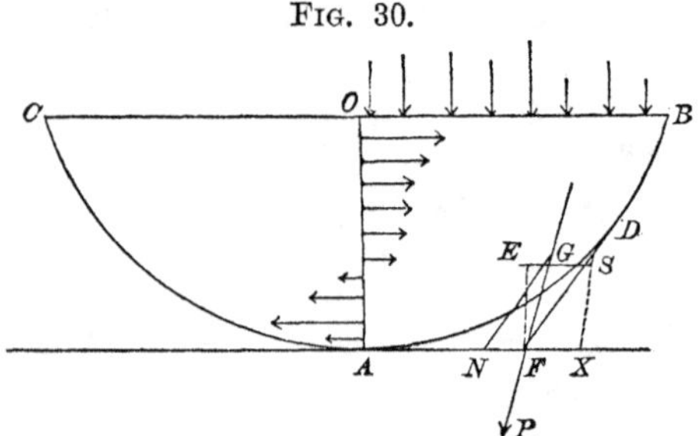

It may often happen that S E $= V \cot i$ $=$ horizontal component of the pull along the cord at D (Fig. 30) is *greater* than G S

$= F\,N = H_0 =$ horizontal pull along the cord at A. In such cases $G\,E = H_0 - V \cot i$ is negative, which indicates that the horizontal load between A and D, for at least a part of this distance, must be contrary in direction to that heretofore discussed; that it must exert an *inward pull* instead of an *outward one* (Fig. 30). If this "inward pull" were removed or replaced by an outward one, the curve would evidently be *flattened* about A.

We may illustrate geometrically, the relation between the forces in all parts of A B.

The vertical load and curve being given draw $F\,E^{V}$ (Fig. 32) = the total vertical load on A B, and lay off on it

$F\,E' =$ vertical load on the arc $A\,D'$.
$F\,E'' =$ " " " $A\,D''$, etc.

Draw a horizontal line at F and lay off F N and F K, each $= H_0$ = pull at A. Draw through F lines parallel to the tangents at $D'\,D''\,D'''$, etc., and through $E'\,E''\,E'''$, etc., lines parallel to the horizon. Then the oblique lines $F\,S'$, $F\,S''$, etc., represent the pulls along the cord at $D'\,D''$, etc., while E′ S′, E″ S″, etc., represent the horizontal components of these pulls. Lay off from each point S′ S″, etc., horizontal lines, each equal to F N, and draw through

FIG. 32.

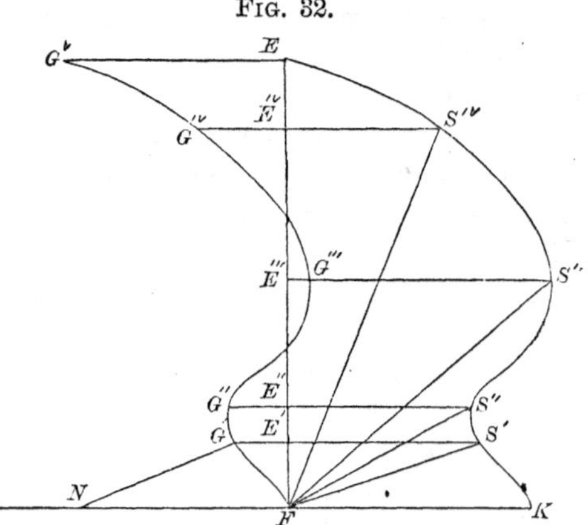

the points G′ G″, etc., thus obtained, a curve. It will evidently be similar to that drawn through K S′ S″, etc., and the line G′ E′ will represent the resultant of the horizontal load that must be distributed along the curve from A to D′ ; G″ E″, the resultant of the horizontal load between A and D″, and so on.

(Fig. 32) is really formed from the parallelogram of forces for the arcs A D′, etc.;

FIG. 31.

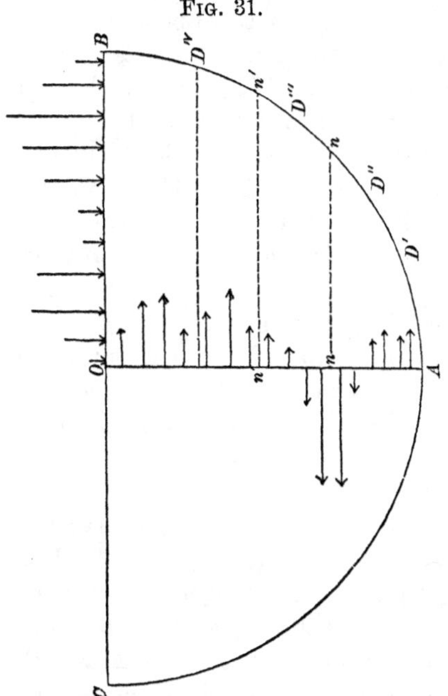

this parallelogram being at D′= F N G′ S′, in which E′ S′ is the horizontal component of the pull at D and E′ G′ = the resultant of the horizontal load on A D′.

As the abscissas of the curve F G′ G″, etc., increase to the left of F E^{V} from the point F to G″ (which correspond to D″ on the curve), the horizontal load acts outward on the arc A D″. The abscissas then diminish to G‴. Hence between D″ and D‴ on the curve, the horizontal load must act inwards as shown in (Fig. 31). From G‴ the abscissas increase until we reach G^{V}. Hence the horizontal load acts outward throughout the remainder of the cord. The points n and n' correspond to those arcs on which the resultant of the horizontal load is zero. Thus on the arc A n the *negative* horizontal load is just equal to the *positive*, and hence their sum = zero. So on the arc A n'.

Note that the abscissas of the curve F G′ . . . G^{V} are not the *intensities* of the horizontal loading, but that each such abscissa represents the *algebraic sum* of the entire horizontal load between A and the point to which the abscissa corresponds. The *intensity* in question has already been shown to be

$$p_x = \frac{d\,H}{dy}.$$

In this expression $d\,H$ = the difference of two neighboring abscissas of the curve F G′. . .G^{v}; as for instance, $d\,H = G'\,E' - G''\,E''$. And dy = vertical projection of the arc D′ D″ of the cord to which the above corresponds.

ARCHES.

FIG. 33.

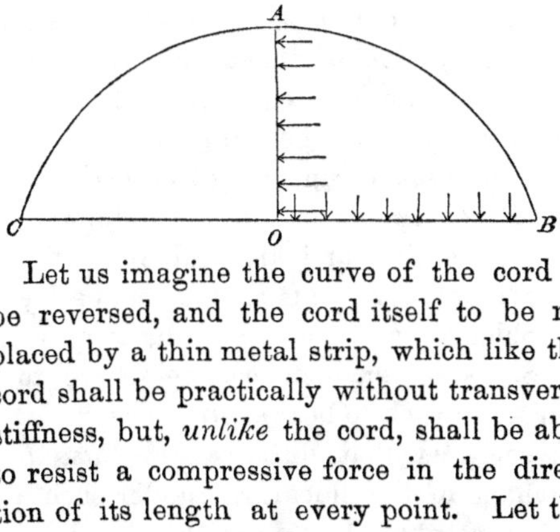

Let us imagine the curve of the cord to be reversed, and the cord itself to be replaced by a thin metal strip, which like the cord shall be practically without transverse stiffness, but, *unlike* the cord, shall be able to resist a compressive force in the direction of its length at every point. Let the loads be distributed as heretofore, except that where there are horizontal components of the load, these should act *inward*, where upon the cord they acted *outward*, and *vice versa*. We then have what is called a "linear arch or rib"; and the curve assumed by it will be identical with that of the cord under equal and similarly distributed loads. If the loading is changed in distribution, the rib will change in shape just as the cord would do under similar circumstances.

In practice there are no "linear arches," but the discussion of them enables us to determine the form of equilibrium for real arches. If we know the form that a *linear arch* would assume under a given load, we can find the "line of pressures" in the real arch. This line and the value of the thrusts at all its points enable us to solve the problems that arise in arch building.

1. Suppose, for instance, we desire to construct an arch to bear a *uniform vertical load*, such as that discussed in *Case I*. The shape of the linear rib under such a load is a parabola. We then as,

1° Step. Assume this curve for the intrados C A B (Fig. 34). If the arch and the load be of homogeneous material, the shape of the *extrados*, or outside of the load,

FIG. 34.

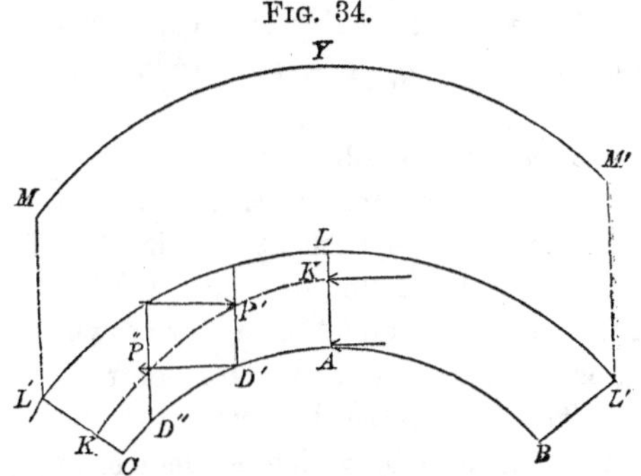

will be M Y M', the vertical distance between C A and M Y being constant.

2° Step. Is to determine the depth A L of the keystone. This depth is always greater than necessary simply to prevent the crushing of the material of the arch under the thrust at the crown. Prof. Rankine's empirical rule derived from the best examples is to make the depth of the keystone in feet

$$\left.\begin{array}{l} \text{In single arches} \\ =\sqrt{.12 \times \text{radius of curva'e at the crown.}} \\ \text{In arches of a series} \\ =\sqrt{.17 \times \text{radius of curva'e at the crown.}} \end{array}\right\} \quad (46.)$$

3° Step. Determine whether the "line of pressures" can lie in the "middle third" of the ring of voussoirs. It should be restricted to the *middle third* to prevent the voussoirs tending to open at any of the joints.

We can test this as follows:

Suppose the voussoirs to be constant in depth all around the arch as in (Fig. 34.) Consider any part of the arch included between the vertical plane (A L) at the crown, and a vertical plane at any other point, as D′ P′. The calculated horizontal thrust along the linear rib, which coincides in shape with the soffit C A, is indicated by the arrow with its head at A. Let the *horizontal thrust* of the rib at D′ be indicated by the arrow with its head at D′ pointing in an opposite direction to that at A. At the crown take A K not greater than $\frac{2}{3}$ A L. Imagine a left-handed couple applied to A L in the vertical plane of the arch, whose force = H = the thrust at A, and whose lever-arm = A K. Apply an equal and opposite couple on the plane D′ P′, with a force H′, equal to the horizontal thrust of the rib at D′. Its lever-arm D′ P′ must then

$$=\frac{H.AK}{H'}$$

In the parabola H = H′ ∴ D′ P′ = A K. These couples being equal and opposite do not change the conditions of equilibrium of the section of the arch L D′, but they transfer the line in which the thrust acts from A D′ to K P. We can repeat the process as often as we choose by taking parts L D″, etc.; and if the curve drawn through the points K P′ P″, etc., lies within the *middle third* of the arch-ring, the arch is sufficiently stable.

In the case before us, the horizontal thrust being constant for every point of the rib C A, the lever-arms D′ P′, D″ P″, etc., are also equal, and therefore the " line of pressures " K K′ is merely the parabola raised vertically a distance = A K. If K K′ does not lie in the *middle third*, a slight increase in the voussoirs, especially towards the springing, will usually remove the difficulty.

4° Step. The joints between the voussoirs,

such as D′ G (Fig. 35) are usually made normal to the soffit A C, but whether this be done or not, the direction of G D′ must be such that at S, where the line of pressures cuts it, the angle included between

FIG. 35.

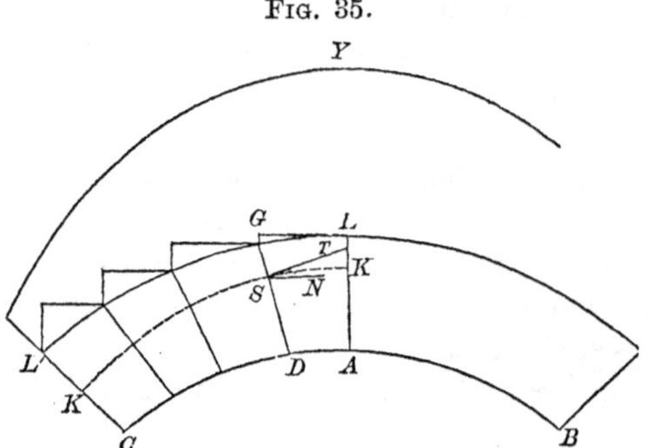

S N (the normal to G D′) and S T (the tangent at S to K K′) may be less than the angle of friction of the material of the voussoirs. The best possible direction for the joints D′ G, etc., would be to make them perpendicular to K K′.

The horizontal component of the thrust (H) along the curve of pressures in a parabolic arch, is, as we have seen, constant; but the thrust along the curve (T) increases

FIG. 36.

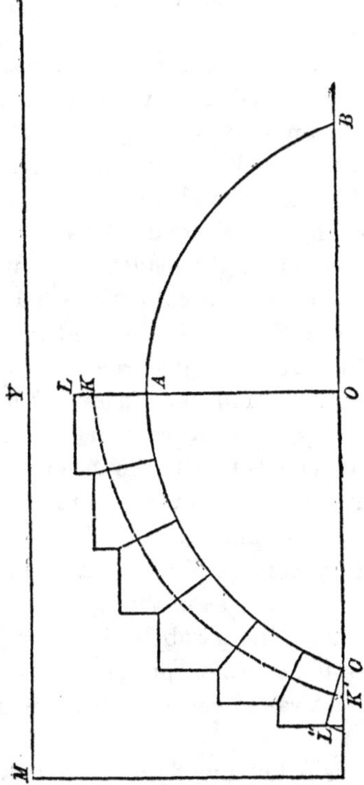

from A to C, and its value at any point may be determined by the formulæ in Case I.

Parabolic stone or brick arches are not common, because it is rare to have such a distribution of the load as that supposed above.

2. But if we reverse the curves discussed under Cases II. and III., we have a form of arch much more frequently applicable.

Thus, suppose the arch and its backing to be homogeneous, and that the *extrados* of this loading is horizontal (M Y), and suppose the action of the load to be entirely vertical. Then the arch and its backing are similar to the metal sheet and the cord discussed in the cases just referred to, and therefore the form of the *linear rib* under such a load will be a catenary or transformed catenary—usually the latter.

Assume this curve for the soffit C A B (Fig. 36); determine the depth A L; the line of the pressures K K′; and the direction of the joints; as in the last case. In this case as in the parabola, H is constant, and hence the curve of pressures is merely the curve C A raised vertically through a distance = A K.

Example. Let the data for a required

arch be (Fig. 37) span C B = 10′; rise O A = 4′; height of extrados M Y above

Fig. 37.

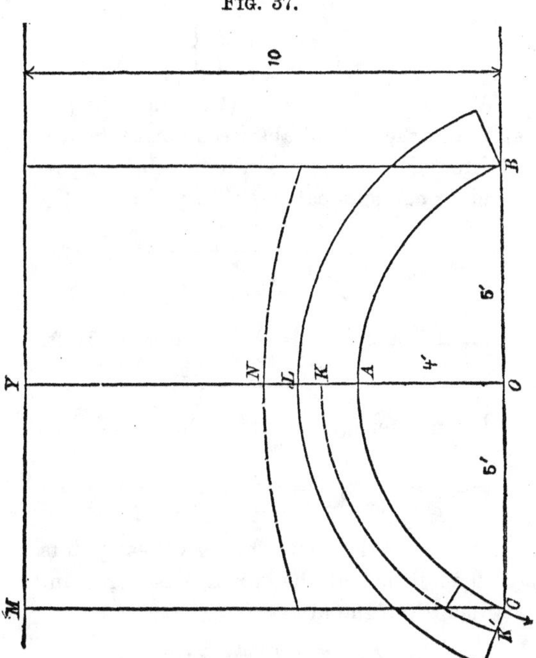

springing at C = 10′. Let the arch and

brickwork be of solid brickwork whose weight w per cubic foot = 112 lbs.

The equation of the transformed catenary passing this C A B is

$$y = \frac{y_0}{2}\left\{ E^{\frac{x}{m}} + E^{-\frac{x}{m}} \right\}$$

Where y_0 = A Y = 6′ (the origin being at Y and the axis of abscissas horizontal).

First find m, the modulus of the corresponding common catenary. By Eq. (14.)

$$m = \frac{x'}{\left\{ \frac{y'}{y_0} + \sqrt{\frac{y'^2}{y_0^2} - 1} \right\}}$$

At the point C $x' = 5$ ft. and $y' = 10$ ft.

$$\therefore m = 4.54 \text{ ft.} = \text{Y N.}$$

Then determine points of the curve, thus for

$x = 1$, $y =$ for $x = 2$, $y =$ for $x = 3$, $y =$ for $x = 4$, $y =$ etc.

Describe the curve through these points.

The thrust at the crown A is (for a unit of length of the arch)

$$\text{H} = w\, m^2 \text{ from Eq. (16).}$$

$$\therefore \text{H} = (112)\,(4.54)^2 = 2308.3 \text{ lbs.}$$

From Eq. (15) area A Y M C =

$$\frac{m y_0}{2}\left\{ E^{\frac{x}{m}} - E^{-\frac{x}{m}} \right\} = 36.32 \text{ sq. ft.}$$

Weight of load A Y M C = P = (112) (36.32) = 4067.84 lbs.

From Eq. (18) thrust at C = T = $\sqrt{P^2+H^2}$ = 4677.1 lbs.

Inclination at C . Tan $i_1 = \frac{d\, y_1}{d\, x_1} = \frac{y_0}{2\, m}$

$$\left\{ E^{\frac{x'}{m}} - E^{-\frac{x'}{m}} \right\} = 1.77.$$

$$\therefore i_1 = 60^\circ\ 32'.$$

The formula for depth of keystone will be satisfied by making the depth of the arch A L = length of one brick = 9″, for this gives 9″ × 12″ = 108 square inches to bear the thrust H = 2308.3 lbs., or T= 4677.1 lbs. The latter is the greatest thrust in the arch.

It is easy to see that K K′ will be in the middle third, for even at C the distance of the point of the curve K K′ vertically over C, from the nearest point of C A, is approximately

$$6 \times \cos\,(90^\circ - 60^\circ\ 32') = 5'' +.$$

The *extrados* of the transformed catenary

need not be the directrix M Y ; it *may* be another transformed catenary *provided these catenaries have the same directrix.*

To illustrate: suppose the weight of a

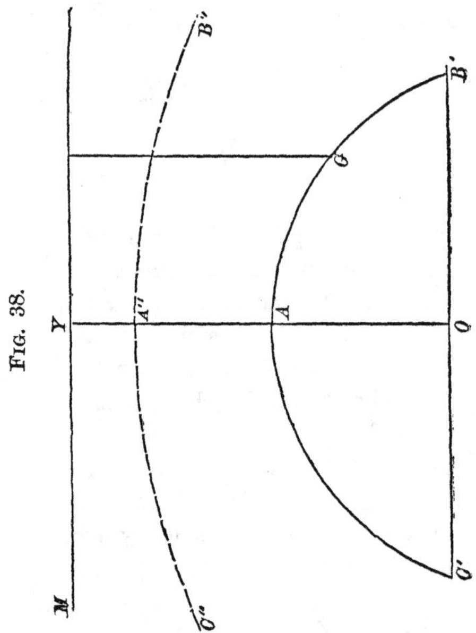

Fig. 38.

unit of the material between CAB and MY $= w$. Then the intensity of vertical pressure at any point G of C A B (Fig. 38) is $=$ $w\,y$. If a heavier building material were used this vertical pressure could be brought upon G by a less height of it. Let this heavier material have a weight per unit $=$ w' and let

$$w' = \frac{2}{3}\,w.$$

Then a column of the heavier material over G and of a height $= \frac{2}{3}\,y$ would give the same pressure as the whole column of the lighter, or

$$w\,y = \frac{2}{3}\,w'\,y \quad . \quad . \qquad (47.)$$

At each point of C A B (Fig. 38) lay off two-thirds of the vertical ordinate, and through these points draw C″ A″ B″. The upper surface of the load may have this form, and yet C A B still be the shape of the linear arch balanced under the applied forces. The equation of C A B being

$$y = \frac{y_0}{2}\left\{ E^{\frac{x}{m}} + E^{-\frac{x}{m}} \right\}$$

that of C″ A″ B″ is evidently

$$y' = \frac{\frac{1}{3}\,y_0}{2}\left\{ E^{\frac{x}{m}} + E^{-\frac{x}{m}} \right\} \qquad (48.)$$

The principle of this example is general.

When the *extrados* is a transformed catenary, note that, since in all the formulæ under Case III., $w =$ the weight corresponding to a unit of surface of the space between C A B and M Y, we must make in these formulæ

$$w = n w'$$

Where $w' =$ weight of the building material and $n = \frac{A A''}{Y A}$.

In arches of this class no provision is needed for horizontal thrust on the spandrels as the arch is equilibrated under vertical loads alone.

In all stone or brick arches, the changes in the curve of pressures K K′ due to passing loads are usually slight, because the weight of such passing loads is generally small compared with the weight of the arch itself and its backing.

3. The simplest practical case in which a uniform normal load (such as that discussed in Case IV.) can be applied to an arch is when it is subjected to water pressure, the arch ring being horizontal instead of ver-

tical. Such a pressure will exist on an empty well constructed in a reservoir or other body of water (Fig. 39). For each

Fig. 39.

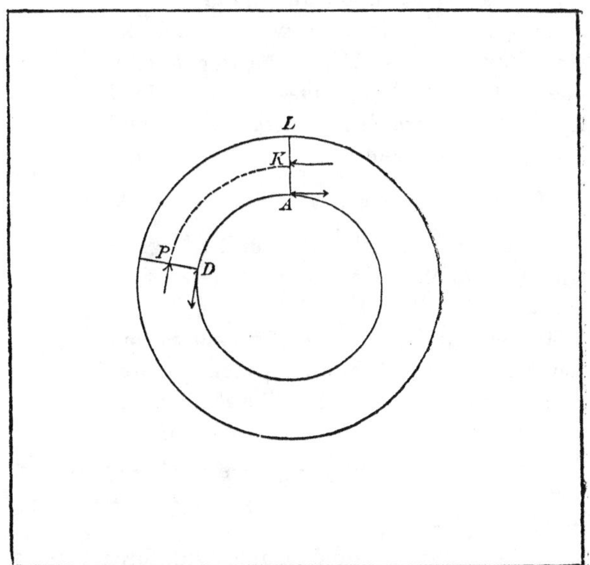

horizontal layer of the well wall may be considered as subjected to a uniform normal pressure of an intensity due to the depth of the water at that layer. This intensity will of course diminish (and so will the pressure on the wall) from one layer to another as we come towards the top.

The soffit of such a well should be *circular* from (Case IV). The thickness of the wall at any depth must be determined by the thrust, which is constant all around any given layer and is

$$T = p\, r = w\, y\, r. \qquad . \quad . \quad (49.)$$

Where w = weight of a unit of water and y = depth of water at the layer in question.

In determining the line of pressures consider a section of the wall between two vertical planes not parallel as heretofore, but both normal to the soffit. Take for the lever-arm of the couple at A (Fig 39) a distance A K = ½ A L. The *force* is still to be = H = T.

At D apply an equal couple with force = the thrust along the soffit at that point, which is also = T = H. Then the lever arm must be equal to A K. Hence we see that the curve of pressures is a circle *parallel* to the soffit and may pass through the middle of the arch ring.

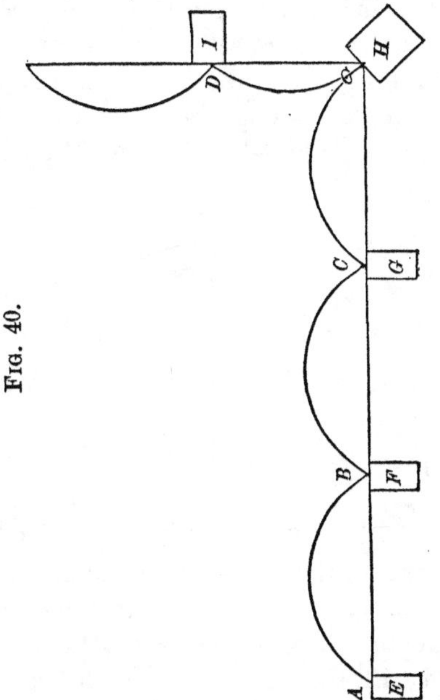

Fig. 40.

This kind of arch may be used for dams or the walls of reservoirs. (See Fig. 40.)

4. There is no case in ordinary practice

where the pressures upon an arch are strictly identical with those on an elliptical cord, for in this case, the pressure must be constant in intensity along both the horizontal and vertical projections of the arch, but the intensity along the *horizontal* must differ from that along the vertical in a constant ratio (Fig. 41). But, as Prof. Ran-

Fig. 41.

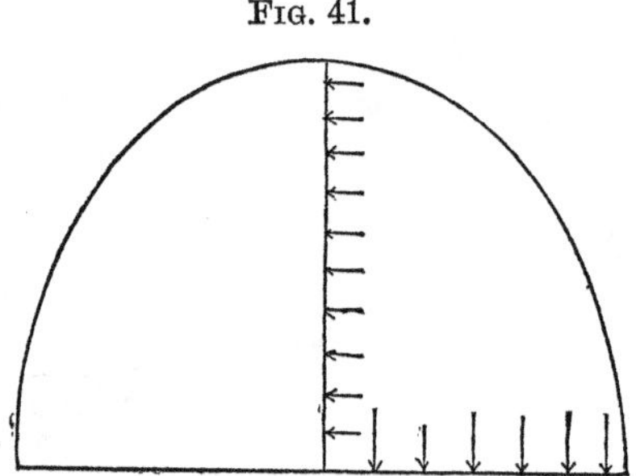

kine says, the curve of equilibrium for the arch of a tunnel through earth, when the depth below the surface is great compared with the rise of the arch itself, approximates to an ellipse.

The pressures in a mass of earth are intermediate in character between those existing in a solid and those in a liquid mass. Thus a little cube of earth (Fig. 42) under the weight of the superincumbent column of earth p, presses downward with a force

Fig. 42.

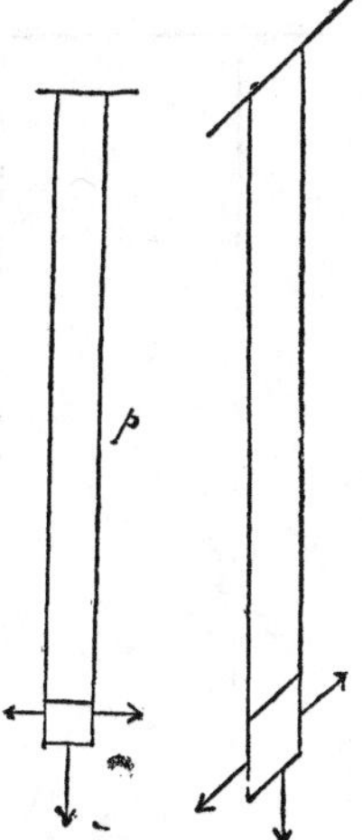

equal to its own weight and that of the column above. It also presses out horizontally with a force *less than this downward force,* but always *bearing a constant ratio to it.* If the little cube were *solid* it would have *no* horizontal push; if *liquid*, that horizontal push would equal its pressure downward. If the upper surface of the earth is

Fig. 43.

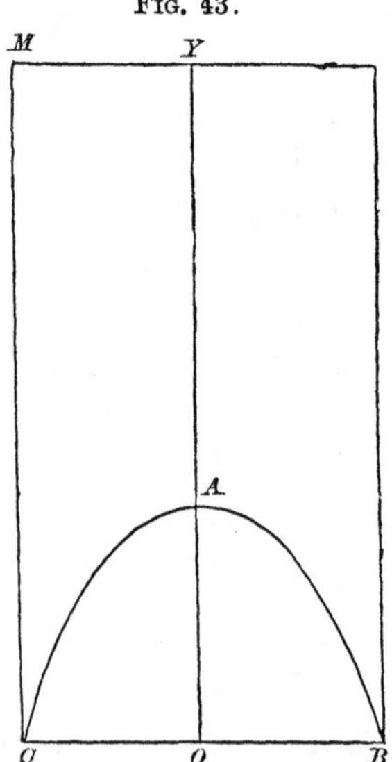

inclined, the outward push which always remains parallel to it becomes inclined too, and is then "conjugate" to the vertical.

If M Y (Fig. 43) is the surface of the earth, when Y A is great compared with A O, then Y A and M C differ so slightly that we may assume them to be equal. We then have on the arch a uniform vertical load whose intensity =

p_y = (Y A) × weight of a unit of the earth = wy_0;

and a horizontal load whose uniform intensity p_x is equal to the vertical intensity (p_y) multiplied by a constant. Let

$$\frac{p_x}{p_y} = c^2 \text{ (a constant).}$$

Then

$$p_x = c^2 wy_0 \text{ and } c = \sqrt{\frac{p_x}{p_y}}.$$

From the discussion of Case V. we see that c must be the ratio of the axes of the ellipse to which the pressures are respectively parallel. Hence if the arch be a semi-ellipse and O B be given, we have

$$\frac{OB}{OA} = c \therefore OA = \frac{OB}{c}.$$

From these data draw the curve of the soffit.

The thrust along the soffit at A

$$= \mathrm{H} = p_y \rho_0 = w y_0 \rho_0 .$$

At C or B it is $\mathrm{V} = p_x \rho_1$.

At other points it may be gotten from eq. (27) Case V.

We can determine the curve of pressures by a method similar to that used in the last case. Here, however, the curve K K′ will not be parallel to C A, since the thrusts along C A are not constant, but increase from A to C. Assume A K (Fig. 44)

Fig. 44.

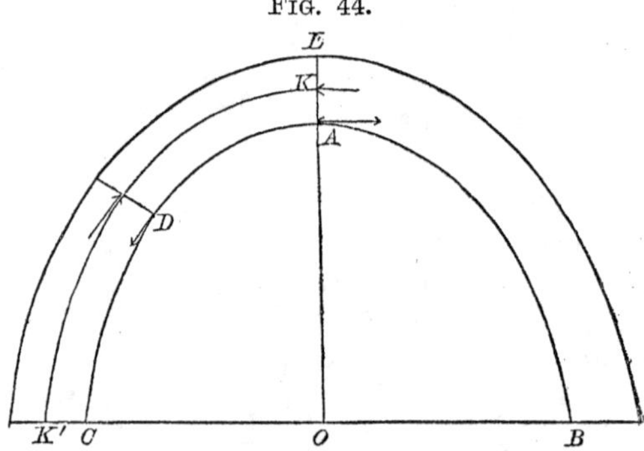

$= \frac{2}{3}$ A L, then the arch must be so proportioned that K K′ shall fall within the middle third.

If the arch C A B is not to be a *semi-ellipse* (as above assumed) but only a *segment* of one, a few trials will enable us to get the ellipse from the data already given.

The strictly true curve of equilibrium required by earth pressure is the Geostatic arch.

5. An arch built with the curve discussed in *Case VI.*, is known as the Hydrostatic arch, from the fact that the loading there described is similar to the pressure of water upon a *vertical* arch.

For if M Y (Fig. 45) be the surface of the water, then its pressure on C A B is normal and proportioned at each point to the depth below M Y. This pressure, as has been shown, may be resolved into a vertical and horizontal pressure at each point, this vertical and horizontal pressure being equal in *intensity* to each other at every point, and also to the normal pressure of which they are the components.

The above form of arch may be applied in two cases.

(1) To bear the pressure of water or other

liquid. Thus in the case of a river tunnel (such as those at Chicago) where the top of

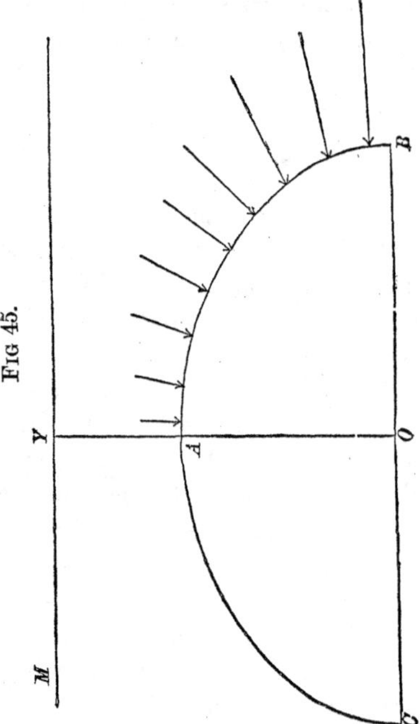

FIG 45.

the tunnel is practically on a level with the bottom of the river, we might use the hydrostatic arch.

The equation of the curve is

$$y\rho = y_0 \rho_0 .$$

The vertical load on the half-arch A B

$$= \int_{x_1}^{0} p dx = \mathrm{V} = w y_1 \rho_1 = \text{thrust along arch at B}.$$

The horizontal pressure against A B

$$= \int_{y_1}^{y_0} p dy = w \frac{y_1^2 - y_0^2}{2} = \mathrm{H} = w y_0 \rho_0 . \quad (51)$$

The thrust along the arch is constant, or

$$\mathrm{T} = \mathrm{H} = \mathrm{V}.$$

The rise A O ($= a$), the depth A Y ($= y_0$), and the radii at A and B (ρ_0 and ρ_1) are connected by the following approximate equations. The co-ordinates of B being x_1 and y_1, let

$$b = x_1 + \frac{x_1^2}{30 a} . \quad \text{Then } y_0 = a \frac{a^3}{b^3 - a^3} \quad (52)$$

$$\rho_0 = \frac{y_1^2 - y_0^2}{2 y_0} = a + \frac{a^2}{2 y_0} = \frac{a}{2} \left(1 + \frac{b^3}{a^3}\right) \quad (53)$$

$$\rho_1 = \frac{y_1^2 - y_0^2}{2 y_1} = a - \frac{a^2}{2 (y_0 + a)} = \frac{a}{2} \left(1 + \frac{a^3}{b^3}\right) . \quad (54)$$

The line of pressures in a hydrostatic arch, since T is constant, is *parallel* to the soffit, as in circular arches.

Example.—Suppose the span to be 50 ft. (Fig. 46) and the depth A Y = 16 ft.

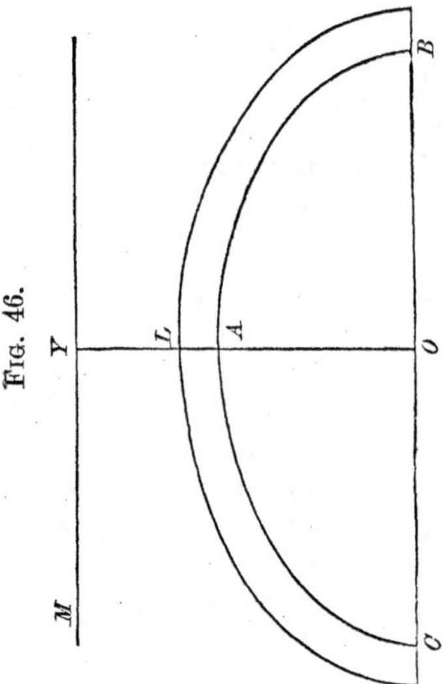

Fig. 46.

Find first the rise A O. In Eq. (52) $x_1 = 25'$ $y_0 = 16'$, and a few trials show that a = rise = 20′ about.

Hence

$$\rho_0 = 32\tfrac{1}{2} \text{ ft. and } \rho_1 = 14.1 \text{ ft.}$$

With these data describe the curve of the

soffit—the radius at any other point besides A and B being given by the equation

$$\rho = \frac{y_0 \rho_0}{y}.$$

The thrust at $A = H = w y_0 \rho_0$. Here $w = 62.4$ lbs.

$$\therefore H = 32448 \text{ lbs.}$$

The rule for the depth of keystone in a single arch gives

Depth A L $= \sqrt{.12 \times 32.5} = 1.9$ ft.

This is ample. It only gives about 120 lbs. per sq. in. as the pressure at the crown.

T being $= H$, the depth of the arch-ring may be uniform.

(2) The hydrostatic arch is also used when the loading is homogeneous masonry up to the extrados M Y, *provided the spandrels be suited to sustain a horizontal thrust at each point of the arch equal to the vertical load at that point.*

As all stone or brick arches sink at the crown when the centres are removed, they will exert at other points an outward horizontal thrust. Now if we assume that this horizontal thrust is at every point equal in *intensity* to the vertical loading at that point, the curve of equilibrium under such a system of forces is the hydrostatic curve. This is the assumed condition of the forces acting in the Neuilly and other bridges of this class.

When the spandrels cannot be made firm and solid this form should not be used, but when they can be, as in the successive arches of a stone bridge, it is advantageous rather than otherwise, to have such a thrust from the arch against the spandrel; while the hydrostatic curve of given span and rise gives a greater *water-way* than the corresponding catenary would.

The catenary needs no resistance from the spandrel, being balanced under the vertical load alone.

Example.—Let the span be 100 ft. and rise 30 ft. Then the depth of loading at the crown (= A Y, Fig. 46) will be found from equation 52

$$= y_0 = 7\tfrac{1}{2} \text{ ft.}$$

Then $\qquad \rho_0 = 91.7 \text{ ft.}$

Hence $H = wy_0 \rho_0$ (putting $w = 160$ lbs.) $= 107600$ lbs.

Depth of keystone

$$= \sqrt{.12 \times 91.7} = 3.3 \text{ ft.}$$

This gives a pressure of 32,280 lbs. to the sq. ft., or about 225 lbs. to the sq. in.

6. If the vertical forces vary as in the hydrostatic arch, and the *horizontal* are not equal to them, but differ at each point in a constant ratio, the curve of equilibrium

FIG. 47.

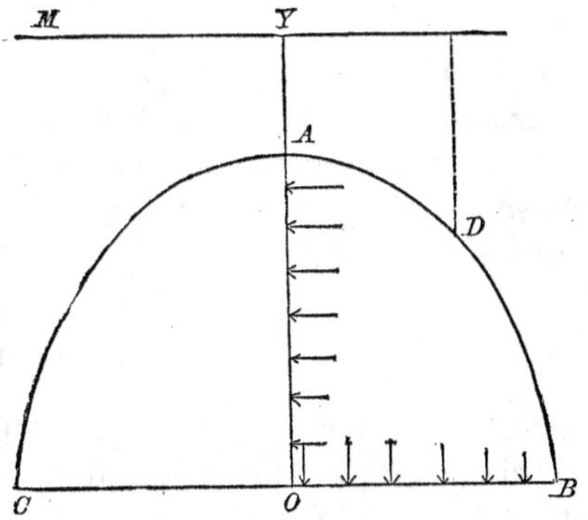

(Fig. 47) becomes the Geostatic curve discussed in *Case VII.* This curve derives its name from the fact, that the system of pressures above described is similar to that exerted by a mass of loose earth against C A B. Let M Y = the horizontal surface of the earth; then at each point D of the arch there is a vertical pressure of intensity (p'_y) proportional to the depth (y) of D below M Y, and a horizontal pressure whose intensity is less than p'_y in a constant ratio,

or $$p'_x = c^2 p'_y$$

(c^2 being taken to represent the ratio of the intensities).

Assume a hydrostatic arch whose vertical dimensions shall be identical with those of the geostatic arch, and whose span (C B) (Fig. 48) shall be connected with the span of the geostatic arch (C′ B′) by the equation

$$C\,B = \frac{C'\,B'}{c}. \qquad (55)$$

The intensity of the vertical pressure (the horizontal is like it) in this hydrostatic arch must be

$$p_y = c p'_y.$$

From these data deduce a hydrostatic arch,

and then pass by parallel projections to the required geostatic arch.

Equations (35) (36) (37) (38) give the values of the quantities needed in discussing the Geostatic arch.

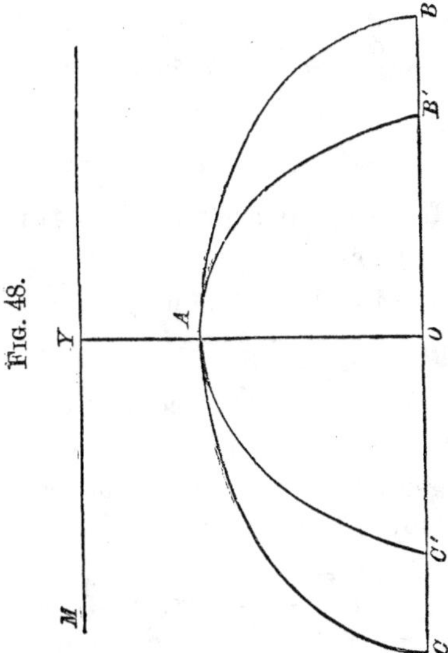

Fig. 48.

Example 1.—Let the span of the geostatic arch ($C' B' = 100$ ft.) be given; also the depth of the loading ($A Y = 20$ ft.);

also the ratio of the pressures ($c^2 = \frac{1}{3}$); and the weight of a cubic ft. of the loading $= w = 100$ lbs. Whence

$$p'_{y_0} = wy_0 = 2000 \text{ lbs.}$$

Then since

$$\text{C B} = \frac{\text{C}'\,\text{B}'}{c} = \frac{100}{\sqrt{\frac{1}{3}}} = 172.4 \text{ ft.}$$

$$cw = 58 \text{ lbs.}$$

$$py_0 = cp'y_0 = \sqrt{\tfrac{1}{3}}\,.2000 = 1154.7 \text{ lbs.}$$

We find from equations (52) (53) (54) for the hydrostatic arch

$$\text{Rise} = a = \text{O A} = 57.7 \text{ ft.}$$

$$\rho_0 = 140.93 \text{ ft.}$$

$$\rho_1 = 36.3 \text{ ft.}$$

$\text{H} = \text{V} = \text{T} = py_0\,\rho_0 = 1154.7 \times 140.93 = 162.700$ lbs. nearly.

In the geostatic arch we have from equations (35 (36) (37) and (38)

Thrust at $\text{B} = \text{V}' = \text{V} = 162700$ lbs.

" $\quad \text{A} = \text{H}' = c\,\text{H} = 94300$ lbs. nearly.

$$\rho_0' = 46.97 \text{ ft.} \quad \rho_1' = 62.65 \text{ ft.}$$

Example 2.—Suppose the span $= 100$ ft. depth, $\text{A Y} = y_0 = 20$ ft. and rise, $a = 30$ ft. given; to find c and thence the hydrostatic arch.

From equation (52) we find

$$b = 40.71,$$

and thence in same equations $x_1 = 39$. Hence the span of the hydrostatic arch

$$= 2x_1 = 78 \text{ ft.}$$

And as c.CB = C′ B′

$$c = \frac{100}{78} = 1.28.$$

Then proceed as in the last example. In this example the hydrostatic arch is the smaller of the two.

The line of pressures in a geostatic arch is found as it was in the elliptic.

The geostatic is the true curve of equilibrium under earth pressure, but when A Y (Fig. 48) is great compared with A O, it approximates the ellipse described through the points C′ A B′ as already stated.

7. Convenience, or other reasons, will often dictate the form of the arch without reference to the loading, and again, necessity may make the vertical load different from any and all the cases we have discussed. In such instances Case VIII. will

enable us to determine the character and amount of the horizontal forces which must be applied through the resistance of the spandrel, when once the form of the arch and the vertical load are known.

When the horizontal forces thus required are *thrusts* directed against the arch, it is

Fig. 50.

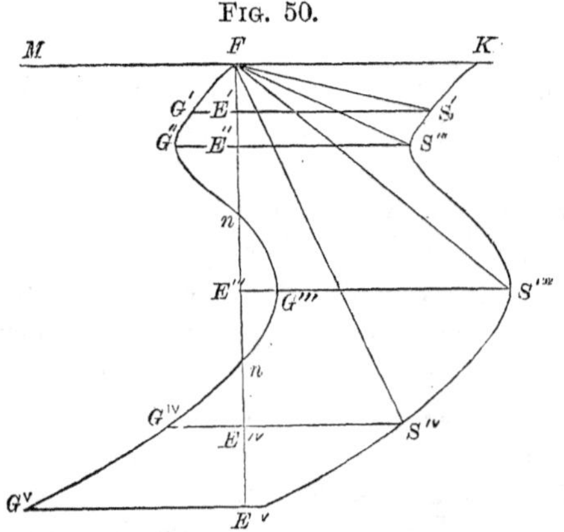

generally possible so to build the spandrel that the arch may be secure, but when they are the opposite, or *outward pulls* on the arch, then it is difficult to insure stability, as to do so requires tension between the arch and the spandrel. In such cases it is best to change the form of the arch.

The discussion of Case VIII. of cords, enables us to determine the necessary data in the case of similar linear arches under similar loads.

Fig. (50) gives the geometrical construction of the triangle of forces at every point of the semi-arch A B (Fig. 49).

We may discuss a given linear arch C A B under a given vertical load, by determining:

1. Thrust at crown; which is

$$H_0 = p_0 \rho_0. \qquad (56)$$

2. Total horizontal thrust required on any arc A D′, A D″, etc. This, from equation (42), is

$$H = H_0 - V \cdot \cot. i. \qquad (57)$$

If this be negative the spandrel must exert a *pull* instead of a thrust.

On the half-arch A B the above equation becomes

$$H_1 = H_0 - V_1 \cot. i_1. \qquad (58)$$

On any arc B D^{IV}, counting from B upwards, the total spandrel thrust is

FIG. 49

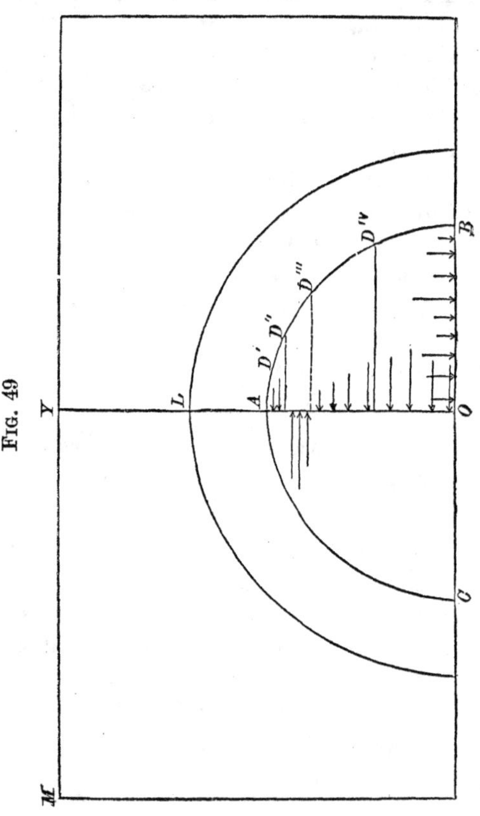

$$H_1 - H = - V_1 \cot. i_1 + V \cot. i. \qquad (59)$$

This last expression has at least one maximum value corresponding to some arc B D. In the Fig. (49) this value corresponds to the arc B D‴.

Let this maximum value be denoted by H_m and let i_m = the inclination at D‴. Then

$$H_m = - V_1 \cot. i_1 + V \cot. i_m = E''' G'''. \qquad \text{(Fig. 50)} \quad (60)$$

D‴ is known as the "point of rupture." There the action of the spandrel ceases to be a thrust, and must, above that point, for some distance at least, become tension.

3. The *intensity* of the horizontal spandrel thrust or pull in any layer (as between D‴ and $D^{\prime v}$) is from equation (43)

$$p_x = - \frac{d\,H}{dy} = - \frac{d\,(V \cot. i)}{dy} = - \frac{d\left(V\,\frac{dx}{dy}\right)}{dy}.$$

When H is positive (that is thrust) p_x is negative, as it should be, since it is equal to the *increment* of the abscissas of the curve F G′ G″, etc. (Fig. 50), and these increments are decreasing from G‴ to G^v.

At the point of rupture

$$p_x = 0. \qquad (61)$$

We can determine the point of rupture in three ways: First, by constructing the Fig. (50) and finding the inclination (i_m) corresponding to the maximum abscissa E''' G'''. Secondly, by substituting the various values of i and V in the value of

$$(H_1 - H) \text{ (eq. 59)},$$

and getting the maximum value of the expression. The i which gives this maximum value corresponds to the point of rupture. Thirdly, by solving equation (61) $p_x = 0$.

4. The thrust along the rib at every point is from equation 40,

$$T = V \text{ cosec. } i, \qquad (62)$$

and it is represented by the inclined lines F S' F S'', etc., Fig. (50).

The *horizontal component* of this thrust is

$$H_r = V \text{ cot. } i = \text{the abscissas of K S', etc.},$$

which are always equal to H_0, the thrust at the crown *minus* the spandrel thrust between A and the point in question

$$\therefore H_r = V \text{ cot. } i = H_0 - H. \qquad (63)$$

This is evidently a maximum at the point of rupture, or, since at the point of rupture,

$$H = H_1 - H_m,$$

we have

$$H_R = H_0 - H_1 + H_m.$$

But

$$H_0 - H_1 = V_1 \text{ cot. } i,$$

$$\therefore \quad H_R = V_1 \text{ cot. } i_1 + H_m. \qquad (64)$$

This horizontal thrust of the rib at D‴ is therefore to be balanced by the horizontal reaction of the abutment at B ($= V_1$ cot. i_1) togther with the resistance of the spandrel between B and D‴ ($= H_m$). When the arch is vertical at B, V_1 cot. $i_1 = 0$.

5. In single arches it is necessary to know the point of application of the resultant of the forces represented by (V_1 cot. $i_1 + H_m$) in order to determine the stability of the abutments. Take moments with reference to the axis of abscissas M Y. Then if $y_R =$ ordinate of point in question, and y_m and y_1 be the ordinates of D‴ and B, we have

$$H_R y_R = (V_1 \text{ cot. } i_1)\, y_1 + \int y d H$$

$$= (V_1 \text{ cot. } i_1)\, y_1 + \int_{y_m}^{y_0} y p_x \, dy.$$

$$y_R = \frac{(V_1 \cot. i_1) y_1 + \int_{y_m}^{y_1} y p_x dy}{H_R}. \qquad (65)$$

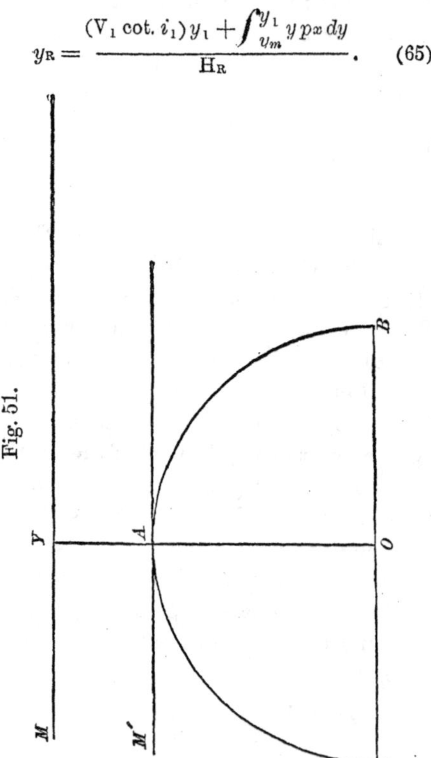

Fig. 51.

In this we neglect the spandrel forces above

D''' so far as they affect the stability of the abutment. This can be done with safety.

The line of pressures and depth of key-stone are determined as heretofore.

Example 1.—Let the assumed form of the soffit be a semi-circle, and let the loading consist of the arch and backing of homogeneous masonry carried up to a horizontal "extrados" M Y (Fig. 51).

Place the radius of the arch $= r$
Depth $AY = ar$
Heaviness of the material $= w$

Take the origin of co-ordinates at A and express the co-ordinates in terms of the inclination i of the arch as on p. 217 *Rankine's C. E.*

Then

$$\text{Thrust at crown} = H_0 = p_0 \rho_0 = (war)\, v = war$$

$$\text{Vertical load on any arc} = V = wr^2 \left\{ (a+1) \sin. i - \frac{\cos. i \sin. i}{2} - \frac{i}{2} \right\}$$

Spandrel thrust on any arc A D

$$H = H_0'' - V \cot. i = wr^2 \left\{ a - (1+a) \cos. i + \frac{\cos.^2 i}{2} + \frac{i \cos. i}{2 \sin. i} \right\}$$

On A B this becomes (since the arch is vertical at B and C)

$$H_1 = war^2 = H_0$$
$$\therefore H_m = V \cot. i_m$$

Intensity of spandrel thrust

$$p_x = -\frac{d(V \cot. i)}{dy} = wr$$
$$\left\{(1+a) - \cos. i - \frac{i - \cos. i \sin. i}{2 \sin^3 i}\right\}$$

The point of rupture is found by putting $p_x = o$ and finding the value of i_m by trials. As a first approximation

$$i_m = \text{arc. cos.} \frac{1 + 3a}{2}$$

Thrust along the rib $= T = V$ cosec i.
At B this is

$$V_1 = wr^2 \left(a + 1 - \frac{\pi}{4}\right).$$

So

$$H_R = V_1 \cot. i_1 + H_m = H_m = wr^2$$
$$\left\{(1+a) \cos. i_m - \frac{\cos.^2 i_m}{2} - \frac{i_m \cot. i_m}{2}\right\},$$

and

$$y_R = \frac{r^2}{H_R} \int_{i_m}^{90^0} p_x \sin. i\,(1 - \cos. i)\,di.$$

Example 2.—Let

$$r = 20' \text{ A Y} = 2\ 5'.$$

Then

$$a = \frac{2.5}{20} = \frac{1}{8} w = 150 \text{ lbs.} \quad \text{(Fig. 52.)}$$

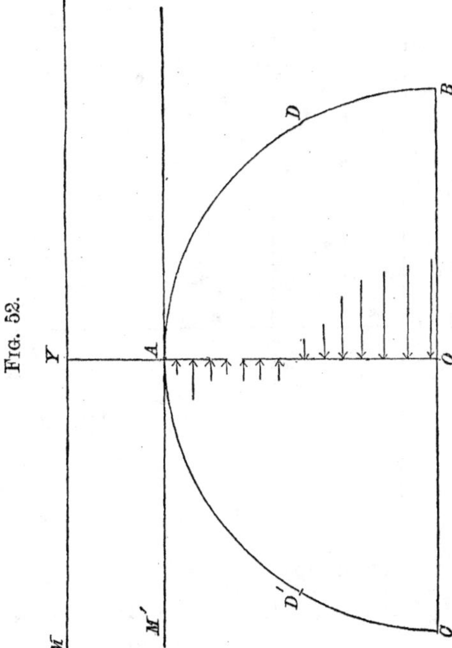

Fig. 52.

Then

$$H_0 = war^2 = 7500 \text{ lbs.}$$

$$V = 60000 \left\{ \frac{9}{8} \sin. i - \frac{\cos. i \sin. i}{2} - \frac{i}{2} \right\}.$$

At B, $V = 60000 \left\{ \frac{9}{8} - \frac{\pi}{4} \right\} = 20376 \text{ lbs}.$

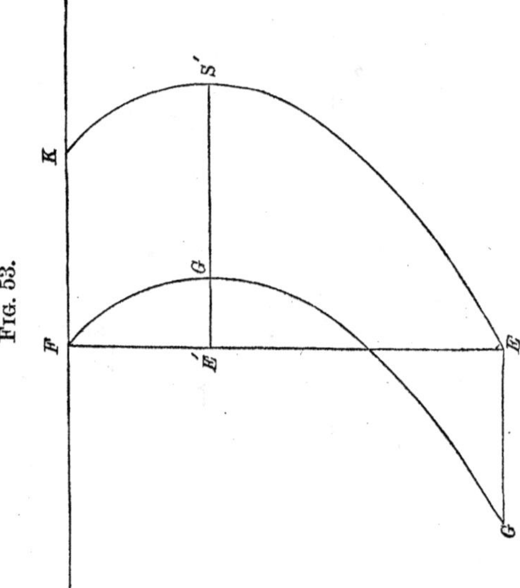

FIG. 53.

Angle of rupture

$$i_m = \text{arc. cos.} \frac{1 + \frac{3}{8}}{2} = \cos.^{-1} .6875 = 46^\circ 34'$$

$$H_R = H_m = 60000$$

$$\left\{ \frac{9}{8} (.6875) - \frac{(.6875^2)}{2} - \frac{.81 \times .947}{2} \right\} = 8154 \text{ lbs.}$$

(Fig. 53) shows the manner in which the forces vary. From A to D (Fig. 52) there must be a pull in the spandrel to produce equilibrium. The total amount of this pull is small, being

$$= 8154 - 7500 = 654 \text{ lbs.}$$

To rid the arch of it, so that the part D^1 A D shall either be balanced under the vertical load alone or exert a thrust outwards, instead of a pull inwards, we *flatten* the arc D^1 A D. A few trials will determine this flattening near enough for practice.

Thus if D^1 A D (Fig. 54) is to be balanced under the vertical load alone, find the centre of gravity of the section D^1 A and its load. Draw a vertical line P through this point, then if we can draw a line from any point in the middle third of the joint D^1 parallel to the tangent to the arch there, and from its intersection with P draw a line parallel to the arch at A which will intersect A L within the middle third, then the extreme points of the line of pressures in the section A D^1 will be within the middle

Fig. 54.

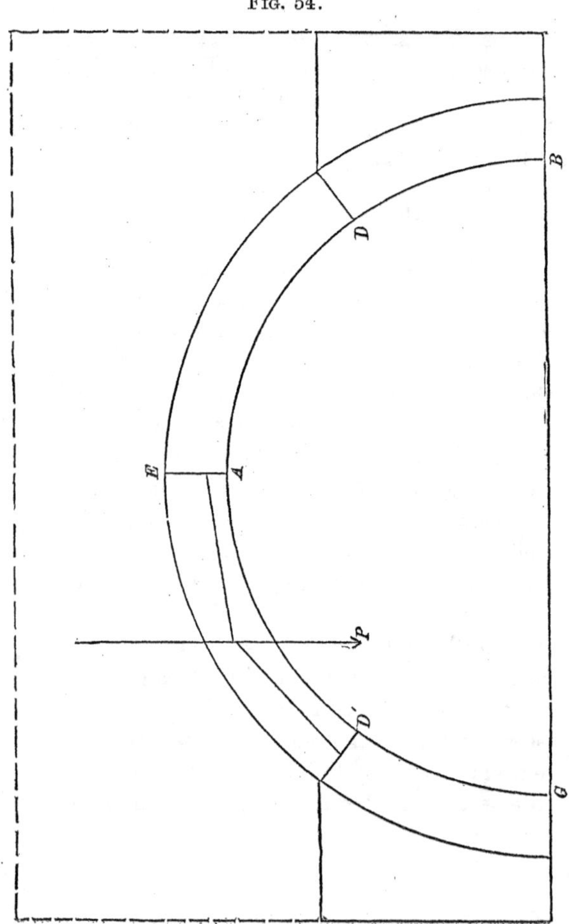

third, and the line of pressures will generally be altogether within it.

The new radius required for the arc D^1 A D may also be determined roughly by putting $H_0 = war^2 = H_R$ and thence getting r^1 since, if D^1 A D is to be balanced under vertical load alone, the horizontal thrust at every point of it must be the same and $= H_R$, the thrust at D^1 and D.

*** Any book in this Catalogue sent free by mail on receipt of price.*

VALUABLE

SCIENTIFIC BOOKS,

PUBLISHED BY

D. VAN NOSTRAND,

23 MURRAY STREET AND 27 WARREN STREET,

NEW YORK.

FRANCIS. Lowell Hydraulic Experiments, being a selection from Experiments on Hydraulic Motors, on the Flow of Water over Weirs, in Open Canals of Uniform Rectangular Section, and through submerged Orifices and diverging Tubes. Made at Lowell, Massachusetts. By James B. Francis, C. E. 2d edition, revised and enlarged, with many new experiments, and illustrated with twenty-three copperplate engravings. 1 vol. 4to, cloth.....................$15 00

ROEBLING (J. A.) Long and Short Span Railway Bridges. By John A. Roebling, C. E. Illustrated with large copperplate engravings of plans and views. Imperial folio, cloth.............................. 25 00

CLARKE (T. C.) Description of the Iron Railway Bridge over the Mississippi River, at Quincy, Illinois. Thomas Curtis Clarke, Chief Engineer. Illustrated with 21 lithographed plans. 1 vol. 4to, cloth 7 50

TUNNER (P.) A Treatise on Roll-Turning for the Manufacture of Iron. By Peter Tunner. Translated and adapted by John B. Pearse, of the Pennsylvania Steel Works, with numerous engravings wood cuts and folio atlas of plates.................$10 00

ISHERWOOD (B. F.) Engineering Precedents for Steam Machinery. Arranged in the most practical and useful manner for Engineers. By B. F. Isherwood, Civil Engineer, U. S. Navy. With Illustrations. Two volumes in one. 8vo, cloth........... $2 50

BAUERMAN. Treatise on the Metallurgy of Iron, containing outlines of the History of Iron Manufacture, methods of Assay, and analysis of Iron Ores, processes of manufacture of Iron and Steel, etc., etc. By H. Bauerman. First American edition. Revised and enlarged, with an Appendix on the Martin Process for making Steel, from the report of Abram S. Hewitt. Illustrated with numerous wood engravings. 12mo, cloth.. 2 00

CAMPIN on the Construction of Iron Roofs. By Francis Campin. 8vo, with plates, cloth........... 3 00

COLLINS. The Private Book of Useful Alloys and Memoranda for Goldsmiths, Jewellers, &c. By James E. Collins. 18mo, cloth........................ 75

CIPHER AND SECRET LETTER AND TELEGRAPHIC CODE, with Hogg's Improvements. The most perfect secret code ever invented or discovered. Impossible to read without the key. By C. S. Larrabee. 18mo, cloth. 1 00

COLBURN. The Gas Works of London. By Zerah Colburn, C. E. 1 vol. 12mo, boards............... 60

CRAIG (B. F.) Weights and Measures. An account of the Decimal System, with Tables of Conversion for Commercial and Scientific Uses. By B. F. Craig, M.D. 1 vol. square 32mo, limp cloth.... 50

NUGENT. Treatise on Optics; or, Light and Sight, theoretically and practically treated; with the application to Fine Art and Industrial Pursuits. By E. Nugent. With one hundred and three illustrations. 12mo, cloth.. 2 00

GLYNN (J.) Treatise on the Power of Water, as applied to drive Flour Mills, and to give motion to Turbines and other Hydrostatic Engines. By Joseph

Glynn. Third edition, revised and enlarged, with numerous illustrations. 12mo, cloth.............. $1 00

HUMBER. A Handy Book for the Calculation of Strains in Girders and similar Structures, and their Strength, consisting of Formulæ and corresponding Diagrams, with numerous details for practical application. By William Humber. 12mo, fully illustrated, cloth.................................... 2 50

GRUNER. The Manufacture of Steel. By M. L. Gruner. Translated from the French, by Lenox Smith, with an appendix on the Bessamer process in the United States, by the translator. Illustrated by Lithographed drawings and wood cuts. 8vo, cloth.. 3 50

AUCHINCLOSS. Link and Valve Motions Simplified. Illustrated with 37 wood-cuts, and 21 lithographic plates, together with a Travel Scale, and numerous useful Tables. By W. S. Auchincloss. 8vo, cloth.. 3 00

VAN BUREN. Investigations of Formulas, for the strength of the Iron parts of Steam Machinery. By J. D. Van Buren, Jr., C. E. Illustrated, 8vo, cloth. 2 00

JOYNSON. Designing and Construction of Machine Gearing. Illustrated, 8vo, cloth.................. 2 00

GILLMORE. Coignet Beton and other Artificial Stone. By Q. A. Gillmore, Major U. S. Corps Engineers. 9 plates, views, &c. 8vo, cloth.................... 2 50

SAELTZER. Treattse on Acoustics in connection with Ventilation. By Alexander Saeltzer, Architect. 12mo, cloth.................................... 2 00

THE EARTH'S CRUST. A handy Outline of Geology. By David Page. Illustrated, 18mo, cloth.... 75

DICTIONARY of Manufactures, Mining, Machinery, and the Industrial Arts. By George Dodd. 12mo, cloth.. 2 00

FRANCIS. On the Strength of Cast-Iron Pillars, with Tables for the use of Engineers, Architects, and Builders. By James B. Francis, Civil Engineer. 1 vol. 8vo, cloth.................................. 2 00

GILLMORE (Gen. Q. A.) Treatise on Limes, Hydraulic Cements, and Mortars. Papers on Practical Engineering, U. S. Engineer Department, No. 9, containing Reports of numerous Experiments conducted in New York City, during the years 1858 to 1861, inclusive. By Q. A. Gillmore, Bvt. Maj -Gen., U. S. A., Major, Corps of Engineers. With numerous illustrations. 1 vol, 8vo, cloth............... $4 00

HARRISON. The Mechanic's Tool Book, with Practical Rules and Suggestions for Use of Machinists, Iron Workers, and others. By W. B. Harrison, associate editor of the "American Artisan." Illustrated with 44 engravings. 12mo, cloth............ 1 50

HENRICI (Olaus). Skeleton Structures, especially in their application to the Building of Steel and Iron Bridges. By Olaus Henrici. With folding plates and diagrams. 1 vol. 8vo, cloth.................... 3 00

HEWSON (Wm.) Principles and Practice of Embanking Lands from River Floods, as applied to the Levees of the Mississippi. By William Hewson, Civil Engineer. 1 vol. 8vo, cloth....................... 2 00

HOLLEY (A. L.) Railway Practice. American and European Railway Practice, in the economical Generation of Steam, including the Materials and Construction of Coal-burning Boilers, Combustion, the Variable Blast, Vaporization, Circulation, Superheating, Supplying and Heating Feed-water, etc., and the Adaptation of Wood and Coke-burning Engines to Coal-burning; and in Permanent Way, including Road-bed, Sleepers, Rails, Joint-fastenings, Street Railways, etc., etc. By Alexander L. Holley, B. P. With 77 lithographed plates. 1 vol. folio, cloth.... 12 00

KING (W. H.) Lessons and Practical Notes on Steam, the Steam Engine, Propellers, etc., etc., for Young Marine Engineers, Students, and others. By the late W. H. King, U. S. Navy. Revised by Chief Engineer J. W. King, U. S. Navy. Twelfth edition, enlarged. 8vo, cloth. 2 00

MINIFIE (Wm.) Mechanical Drawing. A Text-Book of Geometrical Drawing for the use of Mechanics C and Schools, in which the Definitions and Rules of Geometry are familiarly explained; the Practical Problems are arranged, from the most simple to the more complex, and in their description technicalities are avoided as much as possible. With illustrations for Drawing Plans, Sections, and Elevations of Railways and Machinery; an Introduction to Isometrical Drawing, and an Essay on Linear Perspective and Shadows. Illustrated with over 200 diagrams engraved on steel. By Wm. Minifie, Architect. Seventh edition. With an Appendix on the Theory and Application of Colors. 1 vol. 8vo, cloth........... $4 00

"It is the best work on Drawing that we have ever seen, and is especially a text-book of Geometrical Drawing for the use of Mechanics and Schools. No young Mechanic, such as a Machinists, Engineer, Cabinet-maker, Millwright, or Carpenter, should be without it."—*Scientific American.*

—— Geometrical Drawing. Abridged from the octavo edition, for the use of Schools. Illustrated with 48 steel plates. Fifth edition. 1 vol. 12mo, cloth.... 2 00

STILLMAN (Paul.) Steam Engine Indicator, and the Improved Manometer Steam and Vacuum Gauges—their Utility and Application. By Paul Stillman. New edition. 1 vol. 12mo, flexible cloth........... 1 00

SWEET (S. H.) Special Report on Coal; showing its Distribution, Classification, and cost delivered over different routes to various points in the State of New York, and the principal cities on the Atlantic Coast. By S. H. Sweet. With maps, 1 vol. 8vo, cloth..... 3 00

WALKER (W. H.) Screw Propulsion. Notes on Screw Propulsion: its Rise and History. By Capt. W. H. Walker, U. S. Navy. 1 vol. 8vo, cloth..... 75

WARD (J. H.) Steam for the Million. A popular Treatise on Steam and its Application to the Useful Arts, especially to Navigation. By J. H. Ward, Commander U. S. Navy. New and revised edition. 1 vol. 8vo, cloth................................... 1 00

WEISBACH (Julius). Principles of the Mechanics of Machinery and Engineering. By Dr. Julius Weisbach, of Freiburg. Translated from the last German edition. Vol. I., 8vo, cloth.. .... 10 00

DIEDRICH. The Theory of Strains, a Compendium for the calculation and construction of Bridges, Roofs, and Cranes, with the application of Trigonometrical Notes, containing the most comprehensive information in regard to the Resulting strains for a permanent Load, as also for a combined (Permanent and Rolling) Load. In two sections, adadted to the requirements of the present time. By John Diedrich, C. E. Illustrated by numerous plates and diagrams. 8vo, cloth.. 5 00

WILLIAMSON (R. S.) On the use of the Barometer on Surveys and Reconnoissances. Part I. Meteorology in its Connection with Hypsometry. Part II. Barometric Hypsometry. By R. S. Wiliamson, Bvt. Lieut.-Col. U. S. A., Major Corps of Engineers. With Illustrative Tables and Engravings. Paper No. 15, Professional Papers, Corps of Engineers. 1 vol. 4to, cloth.. 15 00

POOK (S. M.) Method of Comparing the Lines and Draughting Vessels Propelled by Sail or Steam. Including a chapter on Laying off on the Mould-Loft Floor. By Samuel M. Pook, Naval Constructor. 1 vol. 8vo, with illustrations, cloth............ 5 00

ALEXANDER (J. H.) Universal Dictionary of Weights and Measures, Ancient and Modern, reduced to the standards of the United States of America. By J. H. Alexander. New edition, enlarged. 1 vol. 8vo, cloth.................................... 3 50

BROOKLYN WATER WORKS. Containing a Descriptive Account of the Construction of the Works, and also Reports on the Brooklyn, Hartford, Belleville and Cambridge Pumping Engines. With illustrations. 1 vol. folio, cloth..........................

RICHARDS' INDICATOR. A Treatise on the Richards Steam Engine Indicator, with an Appendix by F. W. Bacon, M. E. 18mo, flexible, cloth.......... 1 00

POPE. Modern Practice of the Electric Telegraph. A Hand Book for Electricians and operators. By Frank L. Pope. Eighth edition, revised and enlarged, and fully illustrated. 8vo, cloth........................ $2.00

"There is no other work of this kind in the English language that contains in so small a compass so much practical information in the application of galvanic electricity to telegraphy. It should be in the hands of every one interested in telegraphy, or the use of Batteries for other purposes."

MORSE. Examination of the Telegraphic Apparatus and the Processes in Telegraphy. By Samuel F. Morse, LL.D., U. S. Commissioner Paris Universal Exposition, 1867. Illustrated, 8vo, cloth.......... $2 00

SABINE. History and Progress of the Electric Telegraph, with descriptions of some of the apparatus. By Robert Sabine, C. E. Second edition, with additions, 12mo, cloth.............................. 1 25

CULLEY. A Hand-Book of Practical Telegraphy. By R. S. Culley, Engineer to the Electric and International Telegraph Company. Fourth edition, revised and enlarged. Illustrated 8vo, cloth.............. 5 00

BENET. Electro-Ballistic Machines, and the Schultz Chronoscope. By Lieut.-Col. S. V. Benet, Captain of Ordnance, U. S. Army. Illustrated, second edition, 4to, cloth.................................. 3 00

MICHAELIS. The Le Boulenge Chronograph, with three Lithograph folding plates of illustrations. By Brevet Captain O. E. Michaelis, First Lieutenant Ordnance Corps, U. S. Army, 4to, cloth.......... 3 00

ENGINEERING FACTS AND FIGURES An Annual Register of Progress in Mechanical Engineering and Construction, for the years 1863, 64, 65, 66, 67, 68. Fully illustrated, 6 vols. 18mo, cloth, $2.50 per vol., each volume sold separately..............

HAMILTON. Useful Information for Railway Men. Compiled by W. G. Hamilton, Engineer. Fifth edition, revised and enlarged, 562 pages Pocket form. Morocco, gilt....................................... 2 00

STUART. The Civil and Military Engineers of America. By Gen. C. B. Stuart. With 9 finely executed portraits of eminent engineers, and illustrated by engravings of some of the most important works constructed in America. 8vo, cloth.................. $5 00

STONEY. The Theory of Strains in Girders and similar structures, with observations on the application of Theory to Practice, and Tables of Strength and other properties of Materials. By Bindon B. Stoney, B. A. New and revised edition, enlarged, with numerous engravings on wood, by Oldham. Royal 8vo, 664 pages. Complete in one volume. 8vo, cloth....... 15 00

SHREVE. A Treatise on the Strength of Bridges and Roofs. Comprising the determination of Algebraic formulas for strains in Horizontal, Inclined or Rafter, Triangular, Bowstring, Lenticular and other Trusses, from fixed and moving loads, with practical applications and examples, for the use of Students and Engineers. By Samuel H. Shreve, A. M., Civil Engineer. 87 wood cut illustrations. 8vo, cloth............... 5 00

MERRILL. Iron Truss Bridges for Railroads. The method of calculating strains in Trusses, with a careful comparison of the most prominent Trusses, in reference to economy in combination, etc., etc. By Brevet. Col. William E. Merrill, U. S. A., Major Corps of Engineers, with nine lithographed plates of Illustrations. 4to, cloth......................... 5 00

WHIPPLE. An Elementary and Practical Treatise on Bridge Building. An enlarged and improved edition of the author's original work. By S. Whipple, C. E., inventor of the Whipple Bridges, &c. Illustrated 8vo, cloth...................................... 4 00

THE KANSAS CITY BRIDGE. With an account of the Regimen of the Missouri River, and a description of the methods used for Founding in that River. By O. Chanute, Chief Engineer, and George Morrison, Assistant Engineer. Illustrated with five lithographic views and twelve plates of plans. 4to, cloth, 6 00

MAC CORD. A Practical Treatise on the Slide Valve by Eccentrics, examining by methods the action of the Eccentric upon the Slide Valve, and explaining the Practical processes of laying out the movements, adapting the valve for its various duties in the steam engine. For the use of Engineers, Draughtsmen, Machinists, and Students of Valve Motions in general. By C. W. Mac Cord, A. M., Professor of Mechanical Drawing, Stevens' Institute of Technology, Hoboken, N. J. Illustrated by 8 full page copper-plates. 4to, cloth................................ $4 00

KIRKWOOD. Report on the Filtration of River Waters, for the supply of cities, as practised in Europe, made to the Board of Water Commissioners of the City of St. Louis. By James P. Kirkwood. Illustrated by 30 double plate engravings. 4to, cloth, 15 00

PLATTNER. Manual of Qualitative and Quantitative Analysis with the Blow Pipe. From the last German edition, revised and enlarged. By Prof. Th. Richter, of the Royal Saxon Mining Academy. Translated by Prof. H. B. Cornwall, Assistant in the Columbia School of Mines, New York assisted by John H. Caswell. Illustrated with 87 wood cuts, and one lithographic plate. Second edition, revised, 560 pages, 8vo, cloth................................ 7 50

PLYMPTON. The Blow Pipe. A system of Instruction in its practical use being a graduated course of analysis for the use of students, and all those engaged in the examination of metallic combinations. Second edition, with an appendix and a copious index. By Prof. Geo W. Plympton, of the Polytechnic Institute, Brooklyn, N. Y. 12mo, cloth................ 2 00

PYNCHON. Introduction to Chemical Physics, designed for the use of Academies, Colleges and High Schools. Illustrated with numerous engravings, and containing copious experiments with directions for preparing them. By Thomas Ruggles Pynchon, M. A., Professor of Chemistry and the Natural Sciences, Trinity College, Hartford New edition, revised and enlarged, and illustrated by 269 illustrations on wood. Crown, 8vo. cloth........................ 3 00

ELIOT AND STORER. A compendious Manual of Qualitative Chemical Analysis. By Charles W. Eliot and Frank H. Storer. Revised with the Co-operation of the authors. By William R. Nichols, Professor of Chemistry in the Massachusetts Institute of Technology Illustrated, 12mo, cloth....... $1 50

RAMMELSBERG. Guide to a course of Quantitative Chemical Analysis, especially of Minerals and Furnace Products. Illustrated by Examples. By C. F. Rammelsberg. Translated by J. Towler, M. D. 8vo, cloth.. 2 25

EGLESTON. Lectures on Descriptive Mineralogy, delivered at the School of Mines, Columbia College. By Professor T. Egleston. Illustrated by 34 Lithographic Plates. 8vo, cloth........................ 4 50

MITCHELL. A Manual of Practical Assaying. By John Mitchell. Third edition. Edited by William Crookes, F. R. S. 8vo, cloth... .... 10 00

WATT'S Dictionary of Chemistry. New and Revised edition complete in 6 vols. 8vo cloth, $62.00. Supplementary volume sold separately. Price, cloth... 9 00

RANDALL. Quartz Operators Hand-Book. By P. M. Randall. New edition, revised and enlarged, fully illustrated. 12mo, cloth 2 00

SILVERSMITH. A Practical Hand-Book for Miners, Metallurgists, and Assayers, comprising the most recent improvements in the disintegration amalgamation, smelting, and parting of the Precious ores, with a comprehensive Digest of the Mining Laws. Greatly augmented, revised and corrected. By Julius Silversmith. Fourth edition. Profusely illustrated. 12mo, cloth.. 3 00

THE USEFUL METALS AND THEIR ALLOYS, including Mining Ventilation, Mining Jurisprudence, and Metallurgic Chemistry employed in the conversion of Iron, Copper, Tin, Zinc, Antimony and Lead ores, with their applications to the Industrial Arts. By Scoffren, Truan, Clay, Oxland, Fairbairn, and others. Fifth edition, half calf.................... 3 75

JOYNSON. The Metals used in construction, Iron, Steel, Bessemer Metal, etc., etc. By F. H. Joynson. Illustrated, 12mo, cloth............................ $0 75

VON COTTA. Treatise on Ore Deposits. By Bernhard Von Cotta, Professor of Geology in the Royal School of Mines, Freidberg, Saxony. Translated from the second German edition, by Frederick Prime, Jr., Mining Engineer, and revised by the author, with numerous illustrations. 8vo, cloth....... 4 00

URE. Dictionary of Arts, Manufactures and Mines. By Andrew Ure, M.D. Sixth edition, edited by Robert Hunt, F. R. S., greatly enlarged and re-written. London, 1872. 3 vols. 8vo, cloth, $25.00. Half Russia.. 37 50

BELL. Chemical Phenomena of Iron Smelting. An experimental and practical examination of the circumstances which determine the capacity of the Blast Furnace, The Temperature of the air, and the proper condition of the Materials to be operated upon. By I. Lowthian Bell. 8vo, cloth........... 6 00

ROGERS. The Geology of Pennsylvania. A Government survey, with a general view of the Geology of the United States, Essays on the Coal Formation and its Fossils, and a description of the Coal Fields of North America and Great Britain. By Henry Darwin Rogers, late State Geologist of Pennsylvania, Splendidly illustrated with Plates and Engravings in the text. 3 vols., 4to, cloth, with Portfolio of Maps. 30 00

BURGH. Modern Marine Engineering, applied to Paddle and Screw Propulsion. Consisting of 36 colored plates, 259 Practical Wood Cut Illustrations, and 403 pages of descriptive matter, the whole being an exposition of the present practice of James Watt & Co., J. & G. Rennie, R. Napier & Sons, and other celebrated firms, by N. P. Burgh, Engineer, thick 4to, vol., cloth, $25.00; half mor........ 30 00

BARTOL. Treatise on the Marine Boilers of the United States. By B. H. Bartol. Illustrated, 8vo, cloth... 1 50

BOURNE. Treatise on the Steam Engine in its various applications to Mines, Mills, Steam Navigation, Railways, and Agriculture, with the theoretical investigations respecting the Motive Power of Heat, and the proper proportions of steam engines. Elaborate tables of the right dimensions of every part, and Practical Instructions for the manufacture and management of every species of Engine in actual use. By John Bourne, being the ninth edition of "A Treatise on the Steam Engine," by the "Artizan Club." Illustrated by 38 plates and 546 wood cuts. 4to, cloth..$15 00

STUART. The Naval Dry Docks of the United States. By Charles B. Stuart late Engineer-in-Chief of the U. S. Navy. Illustrated with 24 engravings on steel. Fourth edition, cloth.................... 6 00

EADS. System of Naval Defences. By James B. Eads, C. E., with 10 illustrations, 4to, cloth........ 5 00

FOSTER. Submarine Blasting in Boston Harbor, Massachusetts. Removal of Tower and Corwin Rocks. By J. G. Foster, Lieut.-Col. of Engineers, U. S. Army. Illustrated with seven plates, 4to, cloth.. 3 50

BARNES Submarine Warfare, offensive and defensive, including a discussion of the offensive Torpedo System, its effects upon Iron Clad Ship Systems and influence upon future naval wars. By Lieut.-Commander J. S. Barnes, U. S. N., with twenty lithographic plates and many wood cuts. 8vo, cloth..... 5 00

HOLLEY. A Treatise on Ordnance and Armor, embracing descriptions, discussions, and professional opinions concerning the materials, fabrication, requirements, capabilities, and endurance of European and American Guns, for Naval, Sea Coast, and Iron Clad Warfare, and their Rifling, Projectiles, and Breech-Loading; also, results of experiments against armor, from official records, with an appendix referring to Gun Cotton, Hooped Guns, etc., etc. By Alexander L. Holley, B. P., 948 pages, 493 engravings, and 147 Tables of Results, etc., 8vo, half roan. 10 00

SIMMS. A Treatise on the Principles and Practice of Levelling, showing its application to purposes of Railway Engineering and the Construction of Roads, &c. By Frederick W. Simms, C. E. From the 5th London edition, revised and corrected, with the addition of Mr. Laws's Practical Examples for setting out Railway Curves. Illustrated with three Lithographic plates and numerous wood cuts. 8vo, cloth. $2 50

BURT. Key to the Solar Compass, and Surveyor's Companion; comprising all the rules necessary for use in the field; also description of the Linear Surveys and Public Land System of the United States, Notes on the Barometer, suggestions for an outfit for a survey of four months, etc. By W. A. Burt, U. S. Deputy Surveyor. Second edition. Pocket book form, tuck.................................... 2 50

THE PLANE TABLE. Its uses in Topographical Surveying, from the Papers of the U. S. Coast Survey. Illustrated, 8vo, cloth...................... 2 00

"T .s work gives a description of the Plane Table, employed at the U. S. Coast Survey office, and the manner of using it."

JEFFER'S. Nautical Surveying. By W. N. Jeffers, Captain U. S. Navy. Illustrated with 9 copperplates and 31 wood cut illustrations. 8vo, cloth........... 5 00

CHAUVENET. New method of correcting Lunar Distances, and improved method of Finding the error and rate of a chronometer, by equal altitudes. By W. Chauvenet, LL.D. 8vo, cloth................. 2 00

BRUNNOW. Spherical Astronomy. By F. Brunnow, Ph. Dr. Translated by the author from the second German edition. 8vo, cloth...................... 6 50

PEIRCE. System of Analytic Mechanics. By Benjamin Peirce. 4to, cloth.......................... 10 00

COFFIN. Navigation and Nautical Astronomy. Prepared for the use of the U. S. Naval Academy. By Prof. J. H. C. Coffin. Fifth edition. 52 wood cut illustrations. 12mo, cloth 3 50

CLARK. Theoretical Navigation and Nautical Astronomy. By Lieut. Lewis Clark, U. S. N. Illustrated with 41 wood cuts. 8vo, cloth.................... $3 00

HASKINS. The Galvanometer and its Uses. A Manual for Electricians and Students. By C. H. Haskins. 12mo, pocket form, morocco. (In press).....

GOUGE. New System of Ventilation, which has been thoroughly tested, under the patronage of many distinguished persons. By Henry A. Gouge. With many illustrations. 8vo, cloth.................... 2 00

BECKWITH. Observations on the Materials and Manufacture of Terra-Cotta, Stone Ware, Fire Brick, Porcelain and Encaustic Tiles, with remarks on the products exhibited at the London International Exhibition, 1871. By Arthur Beckwith, C. E. 8vo, paper.. 60

MORFIT. A Practical Treatise on Pure Fertilizers, and the chemical conversion of Rock Guano, Marlstones, Coprolites, and the Crude Phosphates of Lime and Alumina generally, into various valuable products. By Campbell Morfit, M.D., with 28 illustrative plates, 8vo, cloth.................................... 20 00

BARNARD. The Metric System of Weights and Measures. An address delivered before the convocation of the University of the State of New York, at Albany, August, 1871. By F. A. P. Barnard, LL.D., President of Columbia College, New York. Second edition from the revised edition, printed for the Trustees of Columbia College. Tinted paper, 8vo, cloth 3 00

—— Report on Machinery and Processes on the Industrial Arts and Apparatus of the Exact Sciences. By F. A. P. Barnard, LL.D. Paris Universal Exposition, 1867. Illustrated, 8vo, cloth.............. 5 00

BARLOW. Tables of Squares, Cubes, Square Roots, Cube Roots, Reciprocals of all integer numbers up to 10,000. New edition, 12mo, cloth................. 2 50

MYER. Manual of Signals, for the use of Signal officers in the Field, and for Military and Naval Students, Military Schools, etc. A new edition enlarged and illustrated. By Brig. General Albert J. Myer, Chief Signal Officer of the army, Colonel of the Signal Corps during the War of the Rebellion. 12mo, 48 plates, full Roan.................................. $5 00

WILLIAMSON. Practical Tables in Meteorology and Hypsometry, in connection with the use of the Barometer. By Col. R. S. Williamson, U. S. A. 4to, cloth.. 2 50

THE YOUNG MECHANIC. Containing directions for the use of all kinds of tools, and for the construction of Steam Engines and Mechanical Models, including the Art of Turning in Wood and Metal. By the author "The Lathe and its Uses," etc. From the English edition with corrections. Illustrated, 12mo, cloth.. 1 75

PICKERT AND METCALF. The Art of Graining. How Acquired and How Produced, with description of colors, and their application. By Charles Pickert and Abraham Metcalf. Beautifully illustrated with 42 tinted plates of the various woods used in interior finishing. Tinted paper, 4to, cloth................ 10 00

HUNT. Designs for the Gateways of the Southern Entrances to the Central Park. By Richard M. Hunt. With a description of the designs. 4to. cloth...... 5 00

LAZELLE. One Law in Nature. By Capt. H. M. Lazelle, U. S. A. A new Corpuscular Theory, comprehending Unity of Force, Identity of Matter, and its Multiple Atom Constitution, applied to the Physical Affections or Modes of Energy. 12mo, cloth... 1 50

PETERS. Notes on the Origin, Nature, Prevention, and Treatment of Asiatic Cholera. By John C. Peters, M. D. Second edition, with an Appendix. 12mo, cloth.. 1 50

BOYNTON. History of West Point, its Military Importance during the American Revolution, and the Origin and History of the U. S. Military Academy. By Bvt. Major C. E. Boynton, A.M., Adjutant of the Military Academy. Second edition, 416 pp. 8vo, printed on tinted paper, beautifully illustrated with 36 maps and fine engravings, chiefly from photographs taken on the spot by the author. Extra cloth.. $3 50

WOOD. West Point Scrap Book, being a collection of Legends, Stories, Songs, etc., of the U. S. Military Academy. By Lieut. O. E. Wood, U. S. A. Illustrated by 69 engravings and a copperplate map. Beautifully printed on tinted paper. 8vo, cloth..... 5 00

WEST POINT LIFE. A Poem read before the Dialectic Society of the United States Military Academy. Illustrated with Pen-and-Ink Sketches. By a Cadet. To which is added the song, "Benny Havens, oh!" oblong 8vo, 21 full page illustrations, cloth.......... 2 50

GUIDE TO WEST POINT and the U. S. Military Academy, with maps and engravings, 18mo, blue cloth, flexible.................................. 1 00

HENRY. Military Record of Civilian Appointments in the United States Army. By Guy V. Henry, Brevet Colonel and Captain First United States Artillery, Late Colonel and Brevet Brigadier General, United States Volunteers. Vol. 1 now ready. Vol. 2 in press. 8vo, per volume, cloth.................... 5 00

HAMERSLY. Records of Living Officers of the U. S. Navy and Marine Corps. Compiled from official sources. By Lewis B. Hamersly, late Lieutenant U. S. Marine Corps. Revised edition, 8vo, cloth... 5 00

MOORE. Portrait Gallery of the War. Civil, Military and Naval. A Biographical record, edited by Frank Moore. 60 fine portraits on steel. Royal 8vo, cloth... 6 00

www.ingramcontent.com/pod-product-compliance
Lightning Source LLC
LaVergne TN
LVHW021420110826
845150LV00007B/2013

* 9 7 8 1 4 2 5 5 0 9 1 4 9 *